The Seven Thunders

Curtis Shearer

TEACH Services, Inc.
PUBLISHING
www.TEACHServices.com

World rights reserved. This book or any portion thereof may not be copied or reproduced in any form or manner whatever, except as provided by law, without the written permission of the publisher, except by a reviewer who may quote brief passages in a review.

This book was written to provide truthful information in regard to the subject matter covered. The author assumes full responsibility for the accuracy of all facts and quotations as cited in this book. The opinions expressed in this book are the author's personal views and interpretation of the Bible, Spirit of Prophecy, and/or contemporary authors and do not necessarily reflect those of TEACH Services, Inc.

This book is sold with the understanding that the publisher is not engaged in giving spiritual, legal, medical, or other professional advice. If authoritative advice is needed, the reader should seek the counsel of a competent professional.

Copyright © 2012 TEACH Services, Inc.
ISBN-13: 978-1-57258-782-3 (Paperback)
ISBN-13: 978-1-57258-783-0 (Hardback)
ISBN-13: 978-1-57258-784-7 (ePub)
ISBN-13: 978-1-57258-785-4 (Kindle/Mobi)
Library of Congress Control Number: 2012937883

All scripture quotations are taken from the King James Version Bible.

Published by

Dedication

This book is dedicated first and foremost to my God, who has never let me down. I repeat, never. The Lord snatched me away from the road that leads to destruction and put me on the path of the ransomed.

I also dedicate this book to my parents, Wallace and Jacqueline Shearer. They have encouraged me through thick and thin and recently celebrated their sixtieth wedding anniversary.

Preface

When the Lord comes will He find faith on the earth? There have been many books written about personal experiences with answered prayer. Many people have experienced miracles and dramatic turnarounds in their lives.

Rather than being merely another personal testimony about going from a life of sin to a life of sobriety and morals, this book encourages you to pursue your dreams. A life that pleases God, although beset at times with trouble, will be richly rewarded by Him through the obtaining of the desires of our hearts.

Many wonder what their mission in life is. We have a God-given free will. We must ask. We must choose. The Lord has given us a commission to go into all the world and share His message of love and salvation. In another place He asks, "Who will go?" My challenge to you at the end of this story is the same as at the beginning. What do you want to do with your life, and what are you waiting for?

TABLE OF CONTENTS

Chapter 1	How It All Began	9
Chapter 2	Military Problems	14
Chapter 3	Partying Instead of Studying	19
Chapter 4	Trying to Hide	22
Chapter 5	Searching for the Truth	26
Chapter 6	Dealing With Past Mistakes	31
Chapter 7	First Steps to Making Things Right	37
Chapter 8	Reaching Those Behind Bars	56
Chapter 9	Letting My Light Shine Close to Home	67
Chapter 10	Friends Listen to Friends	70
Chapter 11	Helping Younger Offenders	78
Chapter 12	My Lord and My God	82
Chapter 13	Many Thanks, Lord	98
Chapter 14	God's Sure Promises	108

Chapter 1

HOW IT ALL BEGAN

The big blue church bus stopped in the middle of the street. Several children eagerly climbed aboard. A young, ambitious boy—Curtis Shearer—was among them. That was I. My parents were irreligious at that time, but they had no objections to us attending church. As far as I can remember, it was a Baptist church. At any rate, the two things that stuck with me from those early exposures to truth were Jesus and the Ten Commandments.

I wasn't a particularly troublesome child in my early years. In fact, it seems like I was kind of favored somehow. The mail carrier used to let me ride around the neighborhood with him and help deliver the mail. I don't suppose those kind of things are allowed anymore. I think that the reason people liked me is because I had a very sensitive heart. There was a young girl on the next street who had to spend a long time in a body cast. She got around by lying on a mechanic's "creeper" and moving along kind of like a turtle. I felt so sorry for her. I would go visit her and try to cheer her up. I especially felt sorry for people who were sad or felt sorry for themselves. Actually, at that time I wanted to be a professional clown when I grew up so I could make people laugh. Though that never happened, I did try to say witty or funny things for much of my life to make people laugh. As I grew older, it became more of an effort to get people to like me. It wasn't as simple as making them laugh.

I grew up in the suburbs of Los Angeles in a gang neighborhood. It was called Pellissier Village. We, that is, my friends in the "Village" and I, gave it a different name more in tune with a gang connotation. We called it "Whittier Village Loco" or WVL for short. *Loco* is Spanish for crazy. That was the image we wanted to portray. We inherited the reputation from the older gang members of the neighborhood, but my friends and I got together and decided that we wanted our reputation to be more of a party neighborhood so that we didn't have to fight as much. We were adolescents during the hippy generation of the late '60s and early '70s, so we represented kind of a cross between the two cultures. We drove our low-rider cars, but we were intent on partying. We still had to fight in gang warfare when circumstances demanded it, but I'll get to that later.

As a youngster I occasionally attended a Lutheran church with a godly, health-minded neighbor. Then as an adolescent I more frequently attended a charismatic church with a friend who was required to attend with his parents.

We were of junior high and high school age by this time. We were more interested in the girls at church than religion. Most of the members spoke in "unknown tongues," which was kind of spooky. They tried to get me to do it at a church camp, but thankfully, I didn't catch on. As was so common during that time period, we were already established alcoholics and beginning drug users. We even attended church functions half drunk. We had a stash of beer and wine buried in my friend's backyard. Just before leaving for church with my friend's parents, we would sneak to the backyard and guzzle down as much alcohol as we could stomach in one thrust. It was easier for me to talk to the girls that way. For some reason I was inhibited and shy around girls.

As with my earliest church attendance, I remember very little of what was taught. But one thing I knew for sure; there was a right way and a wrong way, and I was definitely headed the wrong way. One Sunday school teacher, who was my friend's aunt, tried earnestly to reach us with appeals to live for Christ. Sister Mungia would say with her Bible in hand, "This book will keep you from sin, or sin will keep you from this book." At other times she would say, "If we live according to the Bible and it turns out that there is no heaven after all, at least we have lived a good life and can have a clear conscience." We were told to follow Jesus, but we were never told how to do it.

Many times, out of guilt and desperation, I asked Jesus to come into my heart. But the moment would pass and no real, lasting changes ever developed. I had no power to resist temptation. After my moment of repentance, I would plunge back into sin head first.

Lust was the order of the day for me. My mind, weakened by alcohol and drugs and exposed to degrading pictures and stories, was a continual breeding ground of impure thoughts and desires. To this day, the things I looked at and did haunt me. How I look forward to the day they will be forever erased from my memory.

At the age of 15, I begin working at the neighborhood market. I remember the first glass of beer given to me by the proprietor. I went home and endeavored to do my homework, but I couldn't concentrate. I soon started drinking every day. As well as working at the market part time, I became one of the "back room boys." There was a regular crowd of people who would congregate in the back room of the market. Drinking, gambling, and pornography became well-ingrained habits. I was told by the owner, "Drink all you want, eat all you want, as long as you finish your work." Many times I could not finish my work. As I stumbled out of the door, I was admonished, "Come back and finish in the morning."

As part of my duties, I would pick up beer and supplies from the wholesaler. A case of beer was $4.03 and a keg (15 gallons) was $15. So at age 16 or so, I began supplying beer to parties all around town. I would buy it from the wholesaler under the pretense of getting it for my employer. Sometimes about ten of us guys would pitch in and buy a keg all for ourselves. We would take amphetamines ("uppers" or stimulants) so we could keep drinking until it was gone.

I would drink myself into oblivion. Blackouts were common. There was no such thing as "I've had enough." I drank until it was all gone or I passed out. Sometimes I would have to find out from my friends what had happened because I couldn't remember. Many times, even though I could barely walk, I would drive myself home. I vaguely remember one time driving on the freeway at very high speeds playing chase with my friends in another car. We were recklessly weaving in and out of traffic. God and my angel only know why I'm still alive.

Although I graduated from high school with honors and a four-year academic scholarship for California State University, Los Angeles, things were not looking up. I got arrested for drunk driving, and my license was suspended for six months. I squandered away the scholarship by not using it. My mother, bless her heart, had encouraged me to strive for academic excellence. She bribed me into taking outside classes from the regular school curriculum. Actually, my sixth-grade teacher started me off in pursuit of good grades by giving me straight A's on my report card. I didn't think I deserved it, but it started the ball rolling as far as whetting my appetite to try for the best grades possible.

After not taking advantage of the four-year scholarship, I enrolled at Rio Hondo College. It was called "high school on the hill." My goal in life had devolved into wanting to become a millionaire and God's "gift" to women. I enrolled in business classes in order to become a Certified Public Accountant. I had heard they made big money. Unfortunately, I had an average of three hours of homework per night, which was really cutting into my lifestyle. I felt that I was missing out on all the action.

Outside of school, things were getting really wild and out of control. Drugs were everywhere my friends and I turned. The prevalent drug of choice for many of us in those days was the "downers" or the barbiturates. They were actually sleeping pills, but we had no intention of sleeping while under its influence. One had almost no inhibitions while "loaded" on "Reds" as we called them. My friends and I were doing things that were making some people really angry. It wasn't a good situation at all.

I had had a steady girlfriend since my freshman year in high school. I really loved her, or so I thought. In light of all my other bad choices, it is amazing to think, but I respected her so much that I didn't want to have physical relations with her outside of marriage.

One night we were in town and very "loaded" as usual. My friend's cousin was hanging out on the street with us. He had his girlfriend with him. Someone said, "Hey, she knows how to tell fortunes. Let her read your palm." I knew enough from my limited church attendance to steer clear of those kinds of activities, but my will and inhibitions were broken down by the drugs and alcohol. I let her read my palm out of curiosity. She said, "You're going to go away soon for a long time."

I just laughed, adding, "That's ridiculous. I would never leave my girlfriend."

Within the space of about two weeks, I would say, seven of us drinking partners decided we needed to get away for a while to let things cool down in town. We went to see the army recruiter. Each time we went to see him he would run out and buy a case of beer. But this time we were inducted into the army. We joined under the "buddy plan," which meant that they would try to keep us together if we chose the same job or location. For a two-year enlistment you could have your choice of job or location. The job would be dependent upon sufficient qualifications by way of initial exams. By choosing a location, we took a risk of being assigned to an infantry unit, which was the hardest work and offered no beneficial experience for a career after the military. But we were willing to take the risk, because we wanted to see the world.

I wonder at times what would have happened if I had not opened myself up to demonic influence by having my fortune read. Would I have left my girlfriend, or would I have chosen not to enlist with my friends?

Of course, alcoholism was just as rampant in the military, and our vices simply followed us into new surroundings. While the discipline was good for me, I was still immature and weak-willed.

Basic training took place at Fort Ord, California. It was typical, I suppose. There were lots of fights and lots of sneaky, mean tricks played on people. On graduation day we were very excited to be moving on to bigger and better things. Many of the graduates' parents came to enjoy the ceremony. My parents came to see me—they were glad I was finally making something of myself.

We were in our final formation before being released to join our families for lunch in the chow hall, when I suddenly heard my name. "Private Shearer," the sergeant bellowed.

"Yes, drill sergeant," I replied.

"Get rid of that chewing gum," came the order. So I did. I spit it straight out with a loud smacking sound.

"Private Shearer."

"Yes, drill sergeant."

"Report to the chow hall for KP."

Needless to say, I ended up serving my parents lunch instead of eating it with them.

Chapter 2

Military Problems

After graduation we were shipped off to Fort Sill in Oklahoma for advanced individual training. Looking back, I realize that God was watching over me.

One night while stationed at Fort Sill I ventured into a tavern/nightclub called the Purple Bunny. It was a Saturday night, and I was drunk. We had been warned not to enter certain clubs because the local crowd didn't care for the GIs. This was one of them. Being the drunken idiot I was, I tried to talk to a couple of the girls in the place. Naturally, I was put off, so I started walking to the back of the club where there was a poolroom. As I entered the room, I saw a fight taking place by the pool table. They were beating a guy with cue sticks. I must have said something they didn't like because suddenly I was struck in the face. I started swinging with my beer glass still in my hand. When someone from behind broke a beer pitcher over my head, I saw stars and blacked out.

When I came to, a young couple was helping me to their car to take me to the hospital. Those two young people must have been sent from God to save my life. I think of the sacrifice they made by letting me bleed all over the back seat of their car. The patrons from the Purple Bunny had drug my unconscious body outside and left me to bleed to death.

The young couple drove me to the city hospital where I passed out from lack of blood. I was then transferred to the army hospital on base where it took sixty-eight stitches to sew me up. I was called "Patches" for a while after that because of the quantity of stitches on my head. They were going to keep me there for several days for observation. However, on Sunday morning a doctor who was making rounds came into my room and found me pacing the floor. He called for the nurse and said, "What's he doing here?"

"We were told to hold him for a few days for observation," she said.

"Get him out of here," he replied.

After a quick discharge, I was able to finish training with my class, but I was held up as an example of what not to do.

Upon completion of our training program, several of us went to Germany for our first tour of duty. If I had hoped to distance myself from drugs, alcohol, or bad influences by joining the army or going to Germany, I was, unfortunately, sadly mistaken. One night in Germany I was so drunk that I punched a fellow because of a can of tuna fish. He had offered me some of it to eat but had refused my demand to sell me the whole can, so I punched him. Surprisingly, he did not fight back; instead, we both went to bed.

We were sleeping in an open room at the time, and as I slept, the man I had punched came back with a piece of lead-filled pipe to get his revenge. And he would have done it if another fellow had not awoken and prevented him. In the morning when I opened my eyes, the man I had punched was sitting on my chest. I was still under the blankets. Pointing to his black eye, he said, "Do you remember this?"

"No," I said. He then proceeded to give me a reminder I'll never forget. I tried to defend myself as best I could, but his friends were there with baseball bats in case I started to gain the upper hand.

There were other debacles and debaucheries, some of which are too vile to repeat, but it was about this time that I began to realize I had a problem. I was still far from being converted, but God was watching over me. However, mind you, I was still a long ways off from being able to stand up to the temptations surrounding me.

One evening after taking some LSD and smoking some very strong hashish, I couldn't control my thoughts. I began hallucinating. My three friends were there, and suddenly all three pairs of their eyes came out of their heads and were the only thing I could see in front of my face. Their eyes were blood red. I could hear my friends talking—almost every word from their mouths was profanity. I thought, *This must be what hell is like. I've got to get out of here.* My room was downstairs, and it seemed like it took hours for me to get down those stairs. I don't remember what happened after that.

On another occasion I took some LSD before we headed downtown to a big beerfest. I was wearing some new clothes and sandals. My pants were made of a coarse canvas-like material. As the LSD began to influence my mind, I thought, "I'm like Saul on the road to Damascus." Why I thought that, I have no idea. It must have been the sandals, pants, religious background, and the LSD.

I didn't really understand what happened to Saul on the road to Damascus, but like Saul, what happened to me before the next morning was instrumental toward me making a change in myself that I never dreamed of.

The rest of the night at the beerfest consisted of smoking many pipes full of hash and drinking many mugs of beer. When we finally left the beerfest to walk home to the barracks, I was a raving madman. For some reason I was in a hurry to get "home," so I forged ahead of my group of friends. Apparently, I was talking out loud to myself.

Three other GIs, also returning from the beerfest, were walking right in front of me. One of them turned around and told me to shut up. He stood blocking my way. He was big. His two friends were on either side of me. Being the coward I am, I began whistling for my friends. We had a coded whistle, and they came running. A fight ensued. The three GIs who had accosted me had set down the beer mugs they had stolen from the fest. One of my friends, who didn't have anyone to fight with, picked up one of the mugs by the handle and broke it on the ground, resulting in a vicious weapon. I thought that looked like a good idea, so I did it too.

Now I was the odd man out with no one to fight—there were three guys fighting three other guys. I thought to myself, *These guys are beating each other up, and it's all my fault. Maybe I should just break this whole thing up.* So I started yelling and running around swinging the jagged glass handle threateningly. "Break it up, or I'll kill you," I yelled. I didn't want to hurt anyone, but I wanted to scare them away. The next thing I knew, the big guy who had started the trouble was holding his arm, and blood was squirting out of a large gash and getting all over me.

My friends and I took off running. The next morning the Military Police came to arrest me while I was taking a shower. The next thing I knew I was facing a general court-martial and up to five years in prison, not to mention a dishonorable discharge. A night guard had identified me. He had been on his beat at a nearby officer quarters and had witnessed the whole scene. He finished his tour of duty and left for the states before my trial.

The man who got cut nearly bled to death. They sewed all his tendons together as one so he could not move his fingers individually; he could only close his hand with all of the fingers moving simultaneously. After the trial, at which his attending surgeon testified, he was discharged with 70 percent disability coverage.

This was a severe blow to me. I was scared. I didn't want to go to prison. As the day of my trial drew near, I began to call out to God. I said, "God, if You'll get me out of this mess, I'll let you take this 'chip' off my shoulder."

The "chip" on my shoulder was my attitude toward others. I was friendly to those who I thought were cool, but I couldn't care less about everyone else. I wired home and asked my parents to send me my savings. I had been saving up to buy a car when I got out of the service, but I used the money to hire a civilian lawyer. (I didn't trust a court appointed attorney.) The lawyer charged me $1,350. That was a lot of money back in those days.

A few days after I hired my lawyer, I was called to go to the military judicial headquarters on post. A man invited me into his office. His words to me were,

"Someone upstairs must be looking out for you. The government has assigned you a special court martial."

I found out that if the government thought that there was a chance they might lose a case, they didn't want to lose big. Apparently, my lawyer had a successful reputation. So now I was facing a maximum of six months hard labor and a dishonorable discharge. I would be facing one judge instead a panel of nine judges. And as my lawyer soon informed me, "You've been assigned the only honest judge I know of."

But I was still scared. I had cut the guy. I was guilty, and I knew it. I didn't want to go to prison.

Meanwhile I had to gather several character witnesses. Some of my superiors agreed to testify on my behalf. One of my character witnesses was a staff sergeant. He said to me, "See this ring on my finger? The judge wears one of these, too. You don't have anything to worry about." It turns out they were both Masons. But I do not credit their affiliation for the outcome of my trial. I believe God was active in that courtroom.

Finally the day of my trial arrived. A cloud hung over my spirit. I felt that I was soon to be spending my days behind bars. Just prior to my trial, another soldier who was involved in a separate fight, but with similar results, had received the maximum sentence.

The courtroom setting seemed dark and foreboding. Of those who were involved in the fight and called to testify, most of us could not remember much of the event. Fortunately, one of the friends of the injured man had an unusually clear recollection of the conflict. When my turn came to take the stand, I nervously shared what I remembered. The prosecutor drilled me, pinned me down, and tried to get me to confess to aggravated assault of which I was charged. I denied that I had viciously attacked the man, but I admitted that anything could have happened.

Finally, it was time for the judge to retire to his chamber to deliberate the verdict. Suddenly, it began to thunder outside. It was so loud. Just then my lawyer called me off into a side room. After we sat down, he asked me, "How do you feel about going to prison?"

I was shocked. "You told me we would win." I pleaded for reassurance. The thunder was deafening, questions were swirling around in my head, and my heart was pounding.

"Well, I just have to ask you these things," he said.

"I think going to prison would break me," I said.

We returned to the courtroom. The judge came back in, and I was told to stand.

Then the judge stated these fateful words as he hit his gavel down for emphasis: "By the power vested in me, I find you NOT GUILTY!"

The weight that was lifted off my shoulders must have been visible. I was stunned. Not knowing what to do next, my lawyer told me to go back to the judge's chamber and thank him. I did as I was told and managed to choke out a thank you. He said, "Young man, I have given you a second chance. See that you make the most of it." I recognized in the judge's words an echo of the words of Jesus when He told the woman taken in adultery, "Neither do I condemn thee: go and sin no more."

The injured man's friend had told the truth. If he had twisted the story, my life could have turned out very differently. He had stated that his friend had been afraid that someone was going to get hurt by me swinging the broken beer mug around, so he tried to take it away from me. Since he lunged at me first, the judge ruled that I was innocent by reason of self-defense!

I recognized that it must have been God who had influenced the judge to make that decision. I hadn't been serving the Lord, but He had honored my cry for help. Since I had offered to let Him take the "chip" off of my shoulder if He helped me out of my trouble, I let Him do just that. I vowed to be friendly to everyone, instead of being exclusive and hateful toward some people. I felt my whole attitude change, which was only possible with God's help.

I felt lighter and freer, but I still had a drinking and drug problem that I knew wasn't right. I didn't think it was a sin to drink as long as one didn't overdo it. But that was exactly my problem; I had no self-control. I decided to make another deal with God. I told the Lord that if He would take away the guilty feelings I had about smoking hash I would only drink a couple beers to help me go to sleep at night. I explained to God that I needed the drugs to help me cope with military life and being so far from home. I further promised Him that I would stop taking drugs when I was released from the army.

I felt that God was in agreement with the arrangement I had proposed because, sure enough, I didn't feel guilty about smoking hash anymore. You see, the drugs didn't affect me the same way as alcohol. I was like Dr. Jekyll and Mr. Hyde after coming under the influence of alcohol. I would often do things so people would think I was crazy. Worse yet, when I was completely out of my senses, I would do hateful, evil things. One time I kicked a pregnant woman in the stomach. Of course, the next day I didn't remember doing it.

After talking with God, I felt that I had a contract with Him and permission to keep on with my addiction, but with more restraint on my part. God worked with my ignorance and kept drawing me toward His heart of love.

Chapter 3

PARTYING INSTEAD OF STUDYING

I finished my stint of seven more months in Germany and then returned to the Los Angeles area. For the next two years I used the GI Bill to go to college. Unfortunately, drugs and alcohol were still the norm for me. I really wasn't keeping my end of the bargain with God. Now I was snorting heroin. I also began snorting and smoking PCP, angel dust.

One of my classes at college was a creative writing class. The teacher was a self-proclaimed guru. He had long hair and a long beard. He would lecture while sitting cross-legged on top of a table. This man was teaching things that were different than anything I'd ever heard. He claimed to converse with "spirit guides." He led the whole class through meditation exercises with chanting. We would imagine leaving our bodies and looking down on them.

I was drawn right into the teachings of this man, as well as the so-called "masters of wisdom." They taught that the Bible was a beginner's book and that there was wisdom and knowledge far higher than the Bible. My teacher classed himself with Christ but made fun of Jesus because He gave up His life. Sometimes they quoted portions of the Bible, but the interpretations given to them were fanciful. For example: "The mansions that Jesus went to prepare for us represent the chambers of our mind," one person said. They taught that we must transcend dualism if we were ever to become "enlightened."

Sometimes I would attend class so high on drugs that I couldn't remember what went on. The teachings of reincarnation and karma were appealing to me because they eased my burdened conscience about taking drugs and other immoral habits. But one thing I never let go of was the belief that Jesus had paid the ultimate sacrifice for the sins of the world. That may have been the only thing that kept me from going over the edge in fanatical acceptance of all the New Age teachings.

I had a spiritual void, a hunger, if you will, for understanding the "why" of existence. One day I asked my teacher a question. "What is your best story or example of what love is?" His answer was that love is all of the particles of the universe trying to get back together after being separated in the "big bang." Although a lot can be inferred from that idea, that answer didn't satisfy me. There had to be more to the meaning of true love than that.

During another class period, I commented that I thought the Bible said that if one person in a family got saved, the whole family eventually would be saved. I was very stoned that day on heroin and Quaaludes. The teacher retorted, "What are you worried about? You can't even save yourself." My problem was obvious, and of course, he was right—I couldn't save myself.

This teacher was a vegetarian, and he claimed to have gone a whole year without any kind of intimate relationship with a woman. I remember thinking, *This guy is really out of it. I will never be a vegetarian*. I have since realized that we should be careful about what we say we will never do.

While attending college, I picked up a couple of more DUI charges. They both involved wrecks where I had left the scene of the accident. I lost my drivers license for a year as a result of my poor choices. However, this brush with the law did nothing to change my lifestyle. I continued my education and my profligate lifestyle. Now I was starting to inject the heroin. I was put on Antabuse, a medication that produced unpleasant aftereffects if combined with alcohol, to keep me from drinking. Although the medication pushed me to become a heavier drug user, it did cause me to quit my alcohol intake.

I am convinced that alcohol is a far worse substance to be addicted to than drugs. Without the alcohol running through my system at all times, I was able to begin examining my mind. I had never questioned as to why I did the things I did. An alcoholism counselor asked me why I drank, and the question bewildered me. I had no good answer to give him. I did wonder what life would be like to be sober all of the time. I couldn't understand how people could live that way. Nevertheless, without the alcohol, and spurred on by the "self-awareness" aspect of the New Age movement, I began to question all of my actions, feelings, and thoughts. I would keep asking myself why until I got to the core motive of all of my beliefs and resultant behavior.

I believed I was on a spiritual journey. I wanted to know what true love was, and I wanted to become a loving person. About this time I told my father that my only ambition in life was to become a loving person. Without hesitation, he said, "You're crazy." As I look back on what my life represented at that time, I believe his remark was valid.

Around that time I began talking to God. In my quest for truth, love, and the real meaning of life, I asked God to reveal the truth to me and let the errors fall away. I had read a book called *Stranger in a Strange Land* by Robert Heinlein while serving ten days in county jail for one of my DUI convictions and had come across a definition of love, which was the best I'd ever heard. I accepted it and incorporated it into my view of life. It went like this: love is when someone else's happiness is more important to you than your own happiness. I was desperately searching for the meaning of life, but I was having little success in finding answers in the materials I was reading and the people I was associating with.

Chapter 4

Trying to Hide

I tried to keep my addictions hidden from my family, but I was ignorant of how much they knew. One day two friends and I were cutting up an ounce of heroin in my room when there was a knock on my door. It was my father. He wanted to know if I'd seen his hacksaw. He took a close look at me and said, "You don't look right, and I don't smell alcohol. Are you on drugs?"

All I could offer him was a bewildered look. He became very agitated. He pulled out his pocketknife and, upon opening it, tried to hand it to me. He said, "Why don't you just cut me up with this. That's what you're doing to me anyway."

I didn't know what to do, so I left the house and took off down the street. My father then accosted my friends and sent them off amidst a flurry of blows. My mother and sister came to see what the ruckus was about. They discovered the bowl of heroin in the room and flushed the drugs down the toilet. They returned the bowl to my room. There was quite a bit of residue of heroin still on the bowl when I found it, and with a sickening feeling in my stomach, I marched down the street and gave the bowl to a friend of mine. He fed his addiction off the scrapings of the bowl for several days.

The man who owned the heroin was quite upset, but he could hardly blame my parents for their actions. He had also just returned from serving in the army in Germany. He went right out and bought another bag of heroin although in a smaller quantity since he had suffered a severe loss of revenue from the flushing of the ounce. However, that bag of heroin was forcefully taken from him at knifepoint by my brother and another man. He wasn't having much financial success as a drug dealer. Come to find out, he had been dishonorably discharged from the army for selling drugs—his arms looked like pincushions from all of the needle marks.

The confrontation with my father bothered me for a few days, but my drive and passion for drugs had full control over me. Soon I was back to the same routine again.

The angel dust was my favorite drug for mind exploration. I would smoke it and climb on top of the roof and try to write poetry. When I came down from the roof and the drugs, most of the poetry made very little sense. Still, I believed I was on the path to enlightenment.

My least favorite drug was marijuana. Under its influence I would become extremely self-conscious. My conscience would condemn me. I often felt as if my heart would stop beating at any moment, and I would burn in hell forever. But I never refused it in the presence of others for fear of what they might think of me. Besides that, I believed I needed to do what they did so I could get close to them. In this way I thought they would listen to me when I told them of my newfound understanding of truth, love, and the meaning of life. I saw others having problems, and I believed it was because they were too attached to the things of this world. I saw myself as sort of a human sacrifice for my friends. My health was suffering because of the drugs, and I knew it, but I rationalized that I had to do the drugs in order to help my friends.

One day I put an unusually large dose of PCP in a cup of coffee and drank it down. As usual my mind suddenly snapped to focus, and I heard a loud buzzing noise. Everything around me took on a different appearance and meaning. I had sat down to eat supper in the kitchen, but before I could eat more than a few bites, I began to feel lightheaded. I quickly got up to leave. But before I could get out of the back door, my mind jumped to a drug-induced land of make-believe. My brother was on the patio painting a picture. As I exited the house onto the patio, he said, "What's wrong with you?"

Everything appeared so bright and colorful around me that I said, "We're in heaven." I began to take off my clothes; after all, who needs clothes in heaven? My mother suddenly emerged on the scene. She said, "Get him out of here before his father sees him." A friend of mine who was with me took me for a ride in her car. As we drove through the neighborhood, I imagined the neighbors coming out of their houses. They appeared to me as if they were all looking and pointing at me. I believed they wanted to crucify me.

In my drug-induced state, what appeared to be reality to me was far from the truth. But that was life as I knew it at the time.

My teacher at the college had been teaching that honesty is the highest virtue. That idea hit me hard. I had been lying to others as well as lying to myself. I still remember the day I walked out of English class determined to be honest from then on. I went straight to my girlfriend and told her that I had been unfaithful to her and had no intention of stopping. I began telling people the truth about myself. I began telling others what I thought was the truth about them. My life became an open book, and once again I felt as if a great burden had been lifted off of my shoulders.

But I was extremely far from living a virtuous life. I thought that by being honest I was doing the right thing, but I was still involved in so many bad things that weighed me down.

Because of my blurred state of mind, the Lord had to use some very strong methods to get my attention. As I began to share with certain individuals about my new understanding of truth, love, and the meaning of life, it became apparent that God was working to draw me and others into His arms of love. One day as I was sharing with an acquaintance about this concept of love, it suddenly began to thunder. It hadn't been thundering before our conversion, but we both heard the thunder. It sounded as if the thunder had originated from inside the room we were in. Even though we were high, we felt that something extraordinary had just happened.

For me, this was the second experience I had had with thunder that came seemingly out of nowhere. The timing and circumstances made it stand out as more of a supernatural occurrence. The first thunder was at the court-martial. It had happened at a critical moment that seemed to emphasize what was taking place. It was upon hearing the second thunder that I recognized a pattern developing.

Not long after this event, this same friend came over to visit me at my place. I was no longer living at my parents' house. He wanted to buy some PCP or angel dust—he called it "cosmos."

"It's not here," I said. "A girl a few miles away is holding it for me."

He said, "Let's go get some. I'll give you a ride."

We took off in his car, and he began speeding through the neighborhoods going fifty or sixty miles per hour. I thought he was just showing me how well his car ran, but when he started running stop signs without looking either way first, I began to wonder. "Hey, what's wrong?" I asked.

He turned and looked at me with the most hideous look I've ever seen on anyone's face. "I'm all 'cosmosed' out, man," he said.

As I look back on this, I recognize evidence of demonic manifestation. He then ran a red light through a major intersection without looking either way first and screeched around a corner where we needed to turn. In front of us were two police cars crossing the street through an alley, but they didn't notice us as we shot by behind them and screeched around another corner. When we arrived at the girl's house, I told him to stay in the car and not to start it up. I went in the house and told her what was going on. "I want to see," she said.

We went outside to talk to him. He had rammed his car into another one behind him. We didn't want to sell him the drugs because he had clearly already taken too much, and we told him so. He put his hands together and begged us, saying, "Please,

please let me have it." We didn't have much willpower, so we gave in. I stayed there and he took off.

This young man had been in a motorcycle accident earlier in his life that had caused one of his legs to be straight and stiff. I don't know if the pain was too much or if life had gotten him down, but four days after I sold him the drugs he hanged himself in his closet. The death of this man was only one of several people I knew and shared drugs with who took their own lives, not to mention all of the ones who simply died of an overdose.

Looking back on these incidents makes me hate the devil and his ways. As I relate these stories, it is with the intention to demonstrate my Savior's unfailing love and forgiveness of such wickedness.

And yet, I cry out, "Why, Lord? Why have You spared me?" These souls are lost for eternity. I can never make it right for my part in their destruction, only the death of the perfect Son of God could do that, but I can warn others whose feet are treading a similar path. Like Pilgrim in *Pilgrim's Progress*, I hear the fateful words as I look back on my past: "The wages of sin is death. The wages of sin is death …"

But the gift of God is eternal life. The contrast between death and life grows more apparent every time I think of the pit the Lord pulled me out of. I'm so thankful to Jesus! I deserve death, and He gave me life. What wondrous love! The whole earth is full of His glory.

Chapter 5

Searching for the Truth

Not long after my friend hanged himself, I was sharing with another friend about my new understanding of truth, love, and the meaning of life. I told her about the thunder that I and the other young man had heard as I was telling him the same things. Just then it thundered. It had not been thundering previously. Both my friend and myself heard the thunder. It was a sobering experience for us both. This was the third time I had heard thunder.

One day this friend and I were driving around in her car. My head was buzzing from smoking angel dust. But as we passed a movie theater that was showing the movie *Oh God*, I said, "Let's go watch that movie." I don't know why I said that other than I wanted to find out all I could about God, and this seemed like an opportunity to do so. We bought tickets and found seats in the theater just as the movie started. I quickly realized that the movie was making fun of God. Although there may have been some minor aspects of truth about how God works, the overall premise of the movie was to belittle God. I didn't like that, but at that time, I didn't realize that Hollywood could not be trusted as a source that knew anything about God.

My life continued careening forward. One night we threw a bachelor's party for a friend of mine. Most everyone there got very drunk. Revelry and rudeness reached a fervent pitch. Since I was not drinking, I saw the depths of vanity and reckless abandon to which the mind will succumb when loosed from reason. We didn't do anything other than get really intoxicated, but it was the mental attitudes and conversation that was revolting.

The next day was the wedding. I ingested some LSD early that morning and prepared for the day's events. The wedding was at a Catholic church right around the corner. When I entered the church, the ceremony was well under way, and my LSD trip was well under way, too. As I looked upon the scene, so apparently pious, I realized the dichotomy and the hypocrisy between the party the night before and this sacred event. It was also reported that this priest was a wino.

After just a few minutes, I could not constrain myself. I had to get out of there. As I emerged from the church through the double doors into the courtyard, it began to thunder. The strange thing is that it was a clear, sunny day. I spontaneously burst out laughing, because now I knew that God was talking to me through the thunder. I don't know if anyone else heard the thunder, but it was the fourth time I had heard thunder.

The next instance of hearing thunder occurred some days or weeks later. It was a rainy fall night, and my girlfriend and I were returning to her home after spending some time together. We both had the same English teacher, so we both had been learning things that were making us think. As we drove up the street, I had to keep my head cocked sideways in order to see straight. Thanks to the angel dust when I had my head straight, everything appeared sideways.

We pulled over to the curb about a block from her mom's house, and I began to share with her how God had been dealing with me and teaching me about love. At that moment it began to thunder. We both heard it. It hadn't been thundering previous to this. We were both very excited and awed by this experience. That was the fifth time I had heard thunder.

Somewhere around this time I was visiting with a friend of mine at his house. Like me, he had been in the US army and Germany. But unlike me, he had scars all over his chest and abdomen, including a bullet hole where he had shot himself. He told me that he had demons harassing him and telling him to kill himself. He even told me the name of the demon. Apparently, his older sister had given him LSD when he was younger. While his mind was compromised from the effects of the drug, the demons had found an entrance and a willing victim.

This particular time that I was at his house, he said, "You've got to hear this 'underground' tape my sister lent me." There were several of us present to hear this tape. He said, "I'm going to turn out the lights to make the effect more interesting." As the tape began to play, a man started talking about a group called the "Illuminati." He told about their plans to bring about a one-world government. He said the Masons were involved in the plot. The man that was divulging this sinister plot had actually been a part of the group by virtue of having been born into a family that practiced witchcraft. But he had become a Christian and had left his old ways behind. He also said there would be a one-world economy and religion. Back in 1978, that was a shocking revelation to learn of. He told how they would use terror to get the people to beg for law and order no matter what the cost, even if they had to relinquish many of their long-cherished freedoms. He told how they would cut off the food supply to some of the large cities such as Los Angeles. Anarchy would erupt. Martial law would gain total control over every aspect of our lives.

If it weren't scary enough to find out about such a sinister plot, wouldn't you know it, but it began to thunder. It hadn't been thundering previously. But we all heard the thunder. I made a decision right then and there that would alter my life considerably. I decided to get out of Los Angeles! That was the sixth time I had heard thunder. I drove the thirty or so miles that it took to get to my English teacher's home, and I told him, "They're taking over the world. What should we do?"

"Let them have it," he said.

With all that was going on and all my questions and mixed up thoughts, I decided that maybe I needed a change of scenery. I thought that it might be good if I moved to Northern California. I had spent some time up there, and it seemed like a nice area to live. Also I had an old friend in Washington State that I had recently visited.

I decided to head up to Washington again to visit my friend, which would give me time to formulate a plan as to where I would live. On the way we stopped in Oregon to attend a Rainbow Festival gathering in the Umpqua Mountains. At a certain location they had buses shuttling people to the gathering site.

We arrived at night and were told that it had been quite a day. There was a man at the festival with a vile of LSD. If you went up and shook his hand, he would put a drop of "acid" in your eye. Apparently he had given out thousands of doses that day. As we walked around, we came across a big group of people gathered by some others who were beating drums and chanting and dancing and working themselves into a frenzy.

My friend was tired, so he set out his sleeping bag on the ground and crawled in and went to sleep. A little while later two big dogs started fighting right on top of him. He woke up and started yelling, "What's going on?" We almost split our sides laughing.

In the morning the sun came up bright and early. We were told that it had been cloudy and raining since the event started some days prior. There were some sun-worshippers there who, when they saw the sun come up, took off all their clothes and started bowing before the sun.

Like many others, we had come to hear an author who had written some books on the path to enlightenment. His name was Richard Alpert, but he had taken the name Baba Ram Dass. I had read his books. He was heavily involved in LSD experimentation with Timothy Leary. He had been to India and learned under a guru there.

When I saw this man walking around, he was wearing an interstellar propeller cap and sort of an eastern style outfit. I was on LSD that day. Although he had experimented with LSD, this man now taught that you didn't need LSD to reach a higher consciousness. He said you could achieve the same results by meditating. I had tried meditation and chanting, but I lacked the discipline and endurance to tap into the so-called "higher consciousness." I thank God for that now because I might have been taken over by demons masquerading as spirit guides.

When I saw this man, he had his back to me, but I felt irresistibly drawn to him. At that moment, I thought, *If I can but touch the hem of his garment I shall be made whole*. As I approached, for some reason, I stopped short of touching him. I'm thankful about that, too, because that man had a powerful mind that was being controlled by his guru and Satan.

It amazes me as I think back to this time how what little biblical knowledge I knew came to my mind at strange times and in twisted ways. I believe it was Satan trying to get me to associate the truth of God with the lies of the New Age. I see now how the enemy has tried to mix the Bible with spiritism. One thing these people taught was that after you reached enlightenment, you could leave your body and come back to it whenever you wanted to. Then when you were done with it, you could leave it for good and your body would die.

Interestingly enough, I have met charismatic Christians who believe that when you decide that it is time to go to heaven you just leave your body and it dies. Little do they realize that within that belief lies Satan's first and most successful falsehood. He lied to Eve in the Garden of Eden, telling her that she wouldn't really die but that she would enter another plane of existence or intelligence. That plane of existence is thought by some to be heaven or hell. Others think it to be purgatory. Still others think it to be some sort of universal consciousness or reincarnation.

All of these ideas stem from the devil's first lie that we won't really die. God says that the wages of sin is death. The Bible also says that when we die our thoughts perish. We are in an unconscious sleep-like state. We remain that way until we are called forth by God to one of two resurrections. The first resurrection is for the saved who believe in Jesus' sacrifice. That resurrection takes place when Jesus returns in the clouds, which I believe is very near. The second resurrection will take place one thousand years later. This resurrection will include all of the unsaved, those who rejected the mercy and authority of the Lord. At that time, this unfortunate class will receive the just reward of their life of rebellion—eternal destruction.

I'm reminded when I think back on these things that the counterfeit and the true appear very similar at times. But God will never leave a sincere seeker in darkness. Those who seek after truth will discover Jesus' atoning sacrifice on the cross. God will reveal to an honest seeker His death and resurrection and saving grace.

God's truth is not a mixed-up jumble of creeds. Jesus said, "I am the way, the truth, and the life: no man cometh unto the Father, but by me" (John 14:6). Unfortunately,

Satan does everything in his power to confuse people and cloud minds with false ideas. A friend of mine had joined a religious cult in Seattle, and upon visiting him, I discovered a table covered which Bibles of many different religions. The members of the cult said, "We read all of them. Take your pick." They didn't know what they believed, because they tried to believe it all, taking pieces from here and there that they agreed with.

Today millions of young people all over the world are being drawn into the occult via the Harry Potter craze. They have been conditioned slowly over the years to accept the principles of witchcraft. There is skepticism and every wind of doctrine blowing over the whole earth.

I pray for the poor deluded souls who I met at the Rainbow Festival and at my friend's commune so many years ago, and I pray for people today who are being deceived by the ways of this world. Only God knows what it will take if anything to extricate people from the snare they are in.

Chapter 6

DEALING WITH PAST MISTAKES

Upon returning to Los Angeles from Washington, I learned that one of my previous girlfriends was pregnant with my child. She found me in a bar and broke the news to me. I said, "That's nice." But my current girlfriend was planning to move to Northern California with me. I was torn with my sense of responsibility and my desires. Nevertheless, I decided that the right thing to do was stay in Los Angeles, get a job, and raise this child.

Two weeks after my girlfriend moved up north, I was just about to cut my hair and get a job at a truck stop, but I couldn't stand being away from her so I took off up north and left my previous girlfriend pregnant and without any support.

When I met up with my girlfriend, I told her I wanted to live in Washington, and I asked her if she would come with me. She said that I should go ahead, and she would come join me in about three months.

So I moved to Washington in April 1979. I had an old Volkswagen and very little money. Two other friends joined me in hopes of securing a job that another friend had promised us. Unfortunately, the job only lasted two days.

We lived at the sand dunes and then an abandoned dairy before moving to a park. We got kicked out of all of these areas. We were long-haired hippies who were out of place. We ate carp from the lake and onions we found alongside the road. We found soda pop bottles along the road and cashed them in to buy margarine and a loaf of bread from a discount bakery.

We were hungry, so we went in search of other food. With a shotgun we were able to shoot a pheasant, but it was out of season, so we were fined fifty-eight dollars for killing the pheasant and nineteen dollars for each of our cars being off of the road. They also took away our shotgun.

With all these problems and no place to live, one of my friends left to go back to California. However, two of us stuck it out. In fact, we both obtained full-time work.

I was still drinking quite heavily and taking drugs; but at least there was no angel dust around. One day I drank a pitcher of beer (from the pitcher itself) rather rapidly. Once I had guzzled the liquid, I took off walking in search of my boss's house. Before long, I needed to lie down, so I stopped where I was and lay down in someone's front yard. When I woke up, two police were shining lights in my face. The man of the house was saying, "You're lucky I didn't shoot you." They let me go.

On another occasion I downed another pitcher of beer at a local pizza parlor and passed out at my table. I don't remember a thing about that night, but after waking me up, the owner sent me on my way, hoping I wouldn't kill myself or anyone else while driving home.

I believe the Lord had His hand over me because I was still on probation from the courts of California. If I had been arrested, things would not have turned out like they did.

Around that time my girlfriend showed up, and we lived out of a Volkswagen bus for a time. I was changing in subtle ways. I cut my hair and was enjoying earning my own keep.

Meanwhile back in Los Angeles my pregnant girlfriend was preparing for an abortion. It would be her third. She was admitted into the clinic and waiting her turn when counsel from my mother, who was a Christian by that time, came to her mind and she left the clinic. My mother had visited with her and told her that God wanted her to have this child.

We were in communication, and after she decided to have the child, I began sending her money to pay for a midwife to help with the birth. After nine months, the time came, and she gave birth to a precious little girl. We agreed upon a name—Spirit Jeneil Shearer Sunlight. I didn't see my daughter for the first time until her first birthday. It was on that special event that she and her mother came up to Washington for a two-week visit.

****

After about eleven months of steady work, it began to slack off. It was getting cold, and I wasn't used to extremely cold winters. I was used to the warmth of Los Angeles. I was thinking of leaving Washington. What was there to hold me there? I had no roots and the future seemed so uncertain.

Then one evening we were in a tavern visiting with a friend I'd met. This man had been in many different cults over the years. He had been an original Haight-Ashbury, San Francisco hippy. I began telling him about how I had been court-martialed in the army in Germany for nearly killing a man. He thought for a moment; then he said he had a friend who had been in a situation like I was describing. "What's his name?" I asked. When he told me his friend's name, I realized that it was the same guy I had nearly killed.

"Doc, that is the guy I cut."

"You're kidding?" he said.

"No, I'm not," I said.

"Do you remember about a month and a half ago when I took you over to my friend's house on the base and you and he were having a good time getting drunk together? That was the guy you almost killed. It's a good thing he didn't recognize you because he's a biker, carries a loaded gun, and tears up every bar he goes into. But don't worry, I won't tell him. Besides he has since moved to Phoenix."

Now, I didn't believe in coincidence. There had to be a reason I and the man I'd cut years ago had met again, thousands of miles away from our original homes and the place where the incident took place. Suddenly I knew there was a reason I was where I was, so I decided to stick around. Since I was unemployed at the time, I decided I would go to the library and read. It was warm in there, and I'd always been sort of a bookworm. I was still asking God to lead me to the truth and let the errors fall away. I tried to read the Bible, but I could not understand it and had a hard time concentrating.

Then one day while browsing through the trade-a-book paperback section of the library, a book caught my eye. It had a picture of the world on its cover. There were two hands reaching for the world, one from above and one from beneath. It was called *The Great Controversy*. I opened it up and read the chapter titles: Facing Life's Record, The Origin of Evil, Liberty of Conscience Threatened, The Scriptures a Safeguard, The Time of Trouble, God's People Delivered, The Controversy Ended. The titles caught my attention. I clutched the book to my chest. I knew this was the answer to my prayers.

Some months later I was buying eggs in a local health food store, and the owner handed me a little advertisement. The advertisement told of some lectures being given on the book of Revelation. It was already the fourth night of the series, but my girlfriend and I decided to attend.

The meetings were intriguing, so my girlfriend and I attended the rest of them. When they spoke about Saturday being the true Sabbath of the Bible, I believed it because I figured that the majority is usually wrong. When they proved it from the Bible, the matter was settled in my mind. At the end of the seminar, they asked if anyone from the audience wanted to take a public stand for God and the truth. We went forward. The evangelist told my girlfriend and I that we needed to get married. I knew he was right. He offered to pay for the marriage license. My girlfriend didn't want to get married, but I coerced her into doing so by threatening to leave her if she didn't marry me.

As a result, we were married early one Sabbath morning—June 21, 1980—by the local Seventh-day Adventist minister. The minister asked me if I promised to love, honor, and cherish my wife. "I'll try," I said.

"I think it needs to be a stronger commitment than that," he said.

I responded, "I'll try real hard." He reluctantly accepted that. After the ceremony, he gave us a copy of *The Adventist Home*. Whenever I opened that book, I saw myself as I really was and quickly shut it, putting it back on the shelf to gather dust just as my marriage was doing.

In addition to getting married, the evangelist wanted us to be baptized and join the church. The minister was a little older and wiser, and he asked us if we were ready to give up TV and drinking alcohol and doing drugs. "Whoa, wait a minute," I said. "I'm not ready for all that, and you don't need another hypocrite in your church." My wife concurred with me. In spite of the fact that we weren't ready to abandon all of the bad habits and vices in our life, we were still interested in the Bible and a relationship with God.

Because of our desire to learn, the pastor spent several weeks studying the Bible with us. But at one study I became very agitated. *Do these people really believe what they teach?* I wondered. I came very close to going to my room and bringing out my loaded shotgun to point at the pastor's head to see if he would beg me not to kill him. I'm glad I didn't do that.

There were certain principles I learned from the seminar and subsequent studies with the pastor that I attempted in my own strength to follow. For instance, I decided to not drink alcohol on the Sabbath, but I still worked. I would set my beer down at sunset Friday and pick it back up at sunset on Saturday. I also stopped eating unclean meats, and I even stopped taking drugs, at least for a while.

That summer my friend Doc was staying at our place for a few weeks. One day he came home and said, "Hey, guess who's in town?"

I thought only briefly before saying, "Lonnie?" (The guy I'd cut.)

"Yes, guess what else?"

"What?" I said.

"I told him," he replied.

Suddenly I had visions of this guy driving up with guns a-blazing. (We lived out in the country). I said, "What did he say?"

"He said that if he ever met you again he'd probably just shake your hand, because if he didn't have that disability check coming in every month, he doesn't know what he'd do." Once again I felt a big burden lifted off my shoulders.

An additional prayer I began praying in those days was, "Lord, just make sure

I'm ready to meet You before You come." I knew I was far from ready to meet Jesus, and yet to console myself I would think, "Christians need one another so much because they are weak." I was right, but I didn't understand it the right way.

My drinking was as bad as ever, and when drunk, my willpower was nonexistent, so I plunged back into drugs. I was back using a needle to get my fix. To top it off, I read a book called *Five Families*, and I was convinced that I needed more than one wife. But before I could ever carry out my plan, my wife decided to leave me for another man. I could hardly blame her. She'd been a victim of my unbridled lust for many years until her dignity was all but destroyed.

My life was shattered. I remember kneeling down in my lonesome house and saying this prayer, "Lord, I've made a mess of my life. I'm going to let you fill this big empty void in my heart." When I got up from that prayer, everything had taken on a new meaning. Everything seemed bright and cheerful, at least for a few hours. Even though I made that initial surrender to Christ, I was still vulnerable to temptation and so messed up.

The days immediately following our separation were extremely intense for me. I carried a loaded pistol around in case I wanted to end it all. I traded most of our animals for a few bottles of homemade wine. I would go out in the field and yell as loud as I could until the pressure temporarily subsided. I did some other shameful things that I will not mention. I am so thankful to God for His blood that erases the record of these and other wicked deeds for eternity.

After a little while, I returned to attending the Seventh-day Adventist church in our town. There was a new minister at the church, and I felt that he was speaking especially to me in his sermons. As I began reading my Bible again, Jesus came into my life and the devil left. It wasn't until God miraculously delivered me from my alcohol addiction that I really began drinking in large drafts of the Water of Life.

I read in Revelation 10:3 that God spoke seven thunders. I had heard thunder six times. Now I wondered if I would hear the seventh thunder and under what circumstances? More recently I've realized that I have heard the seventh thunder. I hear it whenever I read God's Word. To those lost in sin, God's Word is the sound of thunder (see Exod. 19:16 and John 12:28, 29). But more specifically I hear the thundering of God's mighty power to save when I read Psalm 81:7: "Thou calledst I trouble, and I delivered thee; I answered thee in the secret place of thunder." I first came across this passage at prayer meeting one evening while we were studying the Psalms. I am still overcome with emotion as I read it. I get goose bumps up and down my spine when I get to this part of my life story.

In verse six of the same Psalm, God says, "I removed his shoulder from the burden." I felt as if Jesus had lifted those burdens off my shoulder.

How is it with you, friend? Can you see the hand of omnipotence in your own life? Though circumstances vary, God is drawing every one of His creatures into His arms of love.

The rest of verse six says, "His hands were delivered from the pots." Those pots were the polluted pools of knowledge in the worldly books I was reading. The Bible is the only book we can trust, and it is for beginners and those advanced in their faith. It is a Book that will last forever.

Chapter 7

FIRST STEPS TO MAKING THINGS RIGHT

Before the Lord could entrust me with so weighty a responsibility as chaplain for juvenile hall, county jail, and prison, He had to teach me how to wait, listen, speak, and forgive unconditionally. I have found that very few people know how to really listen. God is still teaching me how to listen. In order to humble my fierce, stubborn pride, the Lord had to use some very strong measures.

You know, those who live to see Jesus come again must all arrive at the same state of purity before that happens, but we will all have different experiences that lead us to that condition. I want to share with you some of the trying experiences God used to refine my character. The end of Psalm 81:7 says, "I proved thee at the waters of Meribah." The waters of Meribah for me involved Moses Lake because of the severe testing of character I experienced there.

Immediately after my conversion, the Lord delivered me from my drug addiction. I started attending church, but I was still drinking alcoholic beverages. No one had proved to me that it was a sin to drink. In my estimation, according to the Bible, it was only a sin to be drunk.

The following event proved to me that if we go directly to God, He will show us our duty. It just so happened that my friend's wife had been converted to Christ about the same time as I. When I first saw her after my conversion, she told me she was trying to quit drinking. I remembered that the Bible said not to let something we do be a stumbling block to someone else, so I prayed to God and said, "Lord, I don't believe it is a sin to use alcohol, but if You want me to quit drinking, please give me a sign."

What followed was one of the quickest answers to prayer I've ever had. It was the next day or so, as I recall, that I was sitting in my trailer. As my custom was in those days, I would read a chapter a day in my Bible. That day I read 1 Corinthians 5:11: "But now I have written unto you not to keep company, if any man that is called a brother be a fornicator, or covetous, or an idolater, or a railer, or a drunkard." I finished the chapter and started to think about what I had just read when suddenly this big picture that was hanging on the wall just to the right of me fell to the floor.

I went over to inspect why it had fallen. Then I remembered my prayer. I had asked God for a sign if He wanted me to stop drinking. I had just read that there are to be no drunkards in the church. Then this picture fell off the wall just after reading that. I said out loud, "That's a good enough sign for me, Lord."

I went over to the cupboard where I had a brand new gallon of wine. I opened it up and poured it down the drain, and I haven't had a drop since. The Lord completely removed the desire for alcohol at that time, which was more than twenty-eight years ago.

I was now free from the grip of drugs and alcohol, and I fell in love with Jesus Christ because He delivered me from these vices. Since that time I have fallen in love with Jesus in deeper, fuller ways as He has broken my heart into smaller fragments by the revelation of His love for me. In fact, the Lord showed me that His love only flows out to others through the cracks of a broken heart. We only receive more of God's love as we impart that love to others. Therefore, I said to God, "Break my heart into the smallest fragments possible." A person who makes this kind of request of God must be ready and willing to be humiliated to the uttermost.

As I turned my life over to God, I decided it was time to make things right with the girlfriend who I had gotten pregnant, so I asked her to marry me so that we could raise Spirit together. Our daughter was three and a half years old at the time. But within one week of our wedding, we discovered that we agreed on very little, and in fact, we didn't care for each other's company.

Stephanie had said she didn't want anymore children before we got married, but she suddenly changed her mind after we were married. I didn't want more children so that quickly became a major source of contention. One day, in a rage, she threw her Bible at me. I began to realize that this was going to be a long, rough road.

We had promised the Seventh-day Adventist minister, before he married us, that we would never bring up the past; that is, how I had abandoned Stephanie while she was pregnant. That promise being broken early on by my wife was the harbinger of things to come. For the next twelve plus years, I experienced a living hell. I'm not saying I was better than my wife, but our life together was anything from happy. I truthfully believe that the situation was just what I needed to purify my character. It was my crucible.

One year after we were married, my wife developed a full-blown case of multiple sclerosis. It came on so fast that within two to three weeks she was immobile and was having trouble swallowing. In my zeal to stay true to natural healing methods, I did not take her to the doctor. Because of her rapid decline, some neighbors took her in for tests while I was at work. That's when we found out it was MS. Of course, the neighbors didn't offer to help me pay the five hundred plus dollar doctor bill. I only made five dollars an hour and with no medical insurance, I was not prepared for the massive medical expenses that followed. After being examined, Stephanie was immediately placed in the hospital. When I came home and discovered what my neighbors had done, I went to the hospital and talked her out of staying there. I then carried her out in front of the dismayed hospital staff and took her home.

Shortly after that her mother showed up while I was at work and put her and Spirit on a plane and took them back to Los Angeles. I didn't see them again for about three months time.

When they came back home, Stephanie was walking again. But it wasn't long before she once again regressed physically. The enemy took advantage of her condition, especially of her mind, which was affected by the disease. As her short-term memory diminished, confusion and sometimes pandemonium broke out in our home—note that pandemonium has the word "demon" in it.

In her pain and weakened mental state, Stephanie would bite, scratch, and scream at me when I tried to care for her personal needs. I felt that my wife was bent on making my life as miserable as possible for the trauma I had caused her when I abandoned her in her pregnancy. But on the flip side, I felt that if I really needed something from her she would have given it to me. That's just one of the ironies of life, I guess.

I recognized that Satan was behind this disease, trying to drive me to discouragement and despair so that I would let go of my hold on Jesus Christ. Fortunately, it had just the opposite effect—it drove me to the Savior. I could not have stood that trial for one hour if it hadn't been for the abiding love of Christ. I committed to holding on tightly to the hem of Christ's garment and not letting go or becoming discouraged by the trials I was facing.

Even though I was determined not to let go of Christ, the stress of caring for my sick wife and receiving abuse from her began to affect my health. My digestive system completely shut down at one point. I could not even digest simple fruit. She would hit me, pull my hair, and spit in my face and food. Once she even threw a sharp knife at me, which stuck in the wall next to me. I learned to stay fully clothed because I never knew when I would be chased out of the house.

But these trials were just what I needed to cement my faith in God's love and stir within me a desire to love God's people as He loved me. I had so much pride that needed to be humbled. Even now, many years later, I'm suffering in others ways that are humiliating, because that demon of pride must constantly be exposed and deposed.

After we had been married for about five years, Stephanie and Spirit left me for eleven months, during which time, I was informed by my wife and mother-in-law that I had incurred biblical grounds for divorce, which they, of course, would have welcomed. The Savior told me to forgive my wife unconditionally and that I was not to divorce her.

When the separation first began, I told God, "Well, if I can't have a wife, then I'm going to have a motorcycle." Within about six or eight months, I had saved enough money to get what I was looking for—a big Harley Davidson. I quickly discovered that God was not going to let me tell Him what I was going to do. The police took away my Harley, and God gave me back my wife. It turned out that the motorcycle had a stolen engine in it. Eventually, I got the bike back, but I was forced to sell it soon afterward.

All of these challenges and problems made it clear to me that the devil was trying to destroy my relationship with my family and God. The following instance is just one example of Satan's plan to attack my family.

I used to pray every morning for God to put a covering over my daughter to protect her, but one morning I forgot to do that. Being a typical morning, my wife was in a tirade. She said that both Spirit and I could go to hell for all she cared. A little while later, Spirit, upon waking up, attempted to get out of bed, but she fell to the floor and could not get up. Her legs would not support her. She started crying and calling for us. When I saw her condition, I said to myself, *What do I do now? I've got two cripples on my hands*. I knew immediately that it was an attack of Satan, so I prayed, but to no avail. She was still unable to get up and walk. I felt that I needed to get Spirit out of the house, so I took her over to some friends and left her there. They were some of the godliest people I knew. They prayed and prayed, and later on that day, by prayer and enlisting Spirit's willpower, my daughter was able to stand and walk again.

I've had people tell me that Spirit was only mimicking her mother and that's why she couldn't walk. They don't understand the nature of the spiritual warfare in our home. You see, Stephanie's mother had been visiting a fortune-teller for years. In fact, the fortune-teller told her that Stephanie was pregnant before Stephanie even knew herself. The influence of Satanic powers will pass down from one generation to the next in a family if the cycle is not interrupted by the power of God.

I hate Satan intensely for what he did to and through my wife. Anyone who doesn't hate Satan has never seen someone close to them tortured to death by his evil ways.

And so the trial continued, day after day, month after month, year after year. The yelling and cursing was not as jarring to me as it was to my daughter. I tried to instruct her as best I could in light of all the bad language she heard.

At night I could not go to sleep until after my wife did because she would try to attack me when I closed my eyes. I was getting about four hours of sleep per night. When she would come at me yelling, cursing, biting, and scratching, I'd ask Jesus to help me answer her with kindness and gentleness. After repeated harassment though, I often lashed back at her in angry or impatient tones. I would immediately realize my sin, confess to her, and go into another room and repent, staying on my knees until the anger, resentment, and impatient feelings had subsided. I would then go back into the living room where Stephanie was, only to face another onslaught. Within a short time I would fail again. Back to the other room I would go and down on my knees I would confess and repent again. Again and again this went on until I learned how to retain the experience I had on my knees when I got up off of my knees. I was learning how to tap into God's power. I was learning how to abide in Jesus.

You see, I discovered that when we repent of our sins and ask Jesus to come into our heart, we receive Him by faith. God also receives us into His heart at that moment according to 2 Corinthians 6:17, "Wherefore come out from among them, and be ye separate, saith the Lord, and touch not the unclean thing; and I will receive you." God's love is constant, but our relationship with Christ is a progressive covenant relationship. We are to be constantly receiving and increasing the measure of the life of Christ, His Spirit, His grace, and His love "till we all come ... unto the measure of the stature of the fulness of Christ" (Eph. 4:13).

God will receive us more fully as we obey Him and follow His commandments. "And having in a readiness to revenge all disobedience, when your obedience is fulfilled" (2 Cor. 10:6). "Though he were a Son, yet learned he obedience by the things which he suffered; and being made perfect, he became the author of eternal salvation unto all them that obey him" (Heb. 5:8, 9). "For whom the Lord loveth he chasteneth, and scourgeth every son whom he receiveth" (Heb. 12:6).

God does not receive us by faith but by our demonstration. While on earth, He said, "If you love me, keep my commandments" (John 14:15). We are not earning anything. God's love is a free gift, but as we obey Him, we become more able to receive and appreciate His gift. If we choose our own way contrary to God's way, even in one instance, we break the intimacy of the relationship we have with God. We are not at that point abiding in Him. We must renew or re-establish the covenant relationship by confession, repentance, and restitution when applicable. Many are born again by asking Jesus into their heart, but they never achieve the experience of abiding in Christ.

How was it that Jesus abode in the Father's love? John 15:10 gives the answer:

"If ye keep my commandments, ye shall abide in my love; even as I have kept my Father's commandments, and abide in his love." We must abide in Christ in order for Him to abide in us. Yet Jesus must come into our heart first in order for us to abide in Him. Here is another condition for us to abide or remain in Him. John 8:29 says, "And he that sent me is with me: the Father hath not left me alone; for I do always those things that please Him."

I cared for my wife as long as I could, but I finally had to place her in a nursing home. About this time my daughter went away to school, and I was confronted with a grinding, unrelenting loneliness. The only remedy I could find was to get away into nature and be alone with God. But this only helped temporarily. Being around other people increased my loneliness because I had no one to share my life with on a personal, intimate level.

I realize that Jesus is supposed to be our "all in all," but He also created us with a need to give and receive human love and affection. I had a few friends who meant a lot to me, but most of them had let me down in one way or another. As another group of friends let me down during my time of need, I was devastated. I realized the truth of the words of the psalmist: "Put not your trust in princes, nor in the son of man, in whom there is no help" (Ps. 146:3). And "I looked on my right hand, and beheld, but there was no man that would know me: refuge failed me; no man cared for my soul" (Ps. 142:4).

I said to God, "Lord, there's got to be more to being a Christian than this." I went to my room and fell on my knees. "God, I'm not getting up off of my knees until I can feel You in and around me." We are told that faith is not feeling and that we're not to follow our feelings, but this does not mean that we're not allowed to seek the feelings associated with God's love and presence.

I began praying for a deeper experience. As I prayed, I remembered a Spirit of Prophecy statement. I dug it out and began reading it back to God, and with my finger on each word, I claimed it as a promise. Here is the statement:

"The Lord draws out the soul in prayer, and gives us to feel His precious love. We have a nearness to Him, and can hold sweet communion with Him. We obtain distinct views of His tenderness and compassion, and our hearts are broken and melted with contemplation of the love that is given to us. We feel indeed an abiding Christ in the soul. We abide in Him, and feel at home with Jesus. The promises flow into the soul. Our peace is like a river, wave after wave of glory rolls into the heart, and indeed we sup with Jesus and He with us. We have a realizing sense of the love of God, and we rest in His love. No language can describe it, it is beyond knowledge. We are one with Christ, our life is hid with Christ in God. We have the assurance that when He who is our life shall appear, then shall we also appear with Him in glory. With strong confidence, we call God our Father" (*The SDA Bible Commentary,* vol. 3, pp. 1147, 1148).

I said, "Lord this is what I want." Well, I waited and waited, and then a song came into my mind. It was a song that a girls' chorus had sung at County Heaven Academy, a self-supporting Adventist school, called "Embrace the Cross."

I pictured Jesus hanging on the cross in front of me, and I was kneeling just at the base of the cross. I wanted to touch Jesus so badly, but I knew I must remain on my knees. As I reached up to touch Jesus, I realized He was out of my reach. The words of the song played in my head: "Embrace the cross that Jesus died on …," so I did just that. In my mind, I put my arms around that rough and splintery cross.

I had my head bowed and it was very quiet and still. I suddenly realized that I had just killed my Best Friend. I had placed Jesus on that cross. My heart was broken, and as I wept, Jesus spoke to my heart and said, "From now on, everything you need comes from Me."

My friends, if your heart has not been broken at the foot of the cross, seek a deeper experience. If you don't hate your life for crucifying the Son of God you need to ask God to show you your need. We all must die to self. If we don't die to self, we cannot live for Christ. Do not take my word for it. Listen to this statement from Spirit of Prophecy: "He who does not abhor himself can not understand the meaning of redemption. To be redeemed means to cease from sin" (*The Review and Herald,* September 25, 1900).

God revealed to me that I had been leaning on the arm of flesh. He also revealed something else to me. I had prayed for a long time that God would help me to walk with Him as Enoch had walked with Him. One day the Lord spoke to my heart, "If you want to walk with me like Enoch did, then start living like Enoch did." I began to research the life of Enoch. It says that Enoch only met with people, even the righteous, at appointed times, and then for only as long as the people were willing to listen to what the Lord had revealed to him. Do you know that all of those who are privileged to live to see Jesus return will have an experience like Enoch? I do not fancy myself to have arrived at an experience with God like Enoch had, but I do have a different motivation for associating with people than I had before God showed me this. Sometimes I'll be visiting with people when God indicates that it's time to leave.

It was about this same time also that the Lord revealed to me that my speech showed that I relied on the arm of flesh more than God. "What should I do, Lord?" I asked. The Lord basically told me to shut up. He told me to keep my mouth shut until I could learn to speak the truth. God told me this by bringing passages of scripture to my mind. I have asked God for specific things and He has given me specific answers right out of the Scriptures on a number of occasions. This time He spoke to me through Psalm 39:1-3. It says: "I said, I will take heed to my ways, that I sin not with my tongue: I will keep my mouth with a bridle, while the wicked is before me. I was dumb with silence, I held my peace, even from good; and my sorrow was stirred. My heart was hot within me, while I was musing the fire burned: then spake I with my tongue."

My friends, have you ever tried holding back your good words as well as your not so good words? It will stir you. And that hot burning sensation is the Lord, who is a consuming fire, burning the dross, the worldliness, from our conversation. The tongue can no man tame, says the book of James. Only the omnipotent power of God Himself can give us victory over our speech. You know, a lot of people like to "joke around," as they call it. They say something untrue for a laugh, and then they say, "Just kidding," or they simply assume that others will know they are kidding around. I'm sorry to say that that was my experience. I thought I needed to make people laugh in order for them to like me. Is there anything wrong with wanting to be liked? No. But the Lord showed me that I was sacrificing and making a mockery of the truth in order to gain the admiration of fickle men and women. Unfortunately, I have fallen in this area many times since the Lord first reproved me, but with time it is getting easier and easier to remain victorious. With Jesus' help, I shall have full victory.

Next, the Lord had to teach me how to listen. We can't listen when we're too busy talking—at least not very well. I've learned that you can answer more questions listening than you can by speaking. I've discovered that few people are good listeners. God is still teaching me how to listen.

In counseling with juveniles, I've found that unlike the people in jail and prison, they are proud, for the most part, of their misdeeds. They will tell you all about their exploits and misdemeanors—sometimes displaying their knife and bullet scars. If you listen long enough to them, more often than not, after they wind down, they will say, "But you know, I'd like to change my life." Whereas, if you interrupt or offer advice before they reach that point, they may not say they need to change.

God used a very unique way to teach me the fundamentals of listening. It was through a man I will simply call Ed. I became acquainted with Ed when someone at church said he knew a guy who had a drinking problem and could use a little help. I volunteered to visit him. When I walked up to Ed's house, he was standing in the front yard. I said, "Are you Ed?" I held out my hand to shake his as I told him my name.

He said, "I don't know you, and I'm not going to shake your hand. Who are you?"

I knew right away that this guy was dead serious and didn't dabble in small talk.

I said, "I'm an ambassador for Christ."

He said, "You're not a cop?"

"No, I'm not," I replied.

He said, "Then I can shake your hand."

Ed was an alcoholic and a drug addict. He rarely ate food; instead, he opted to mostly just drink. A Vietnam veteran, he suffered from post-traumatic stress disorder. He was violent, suicidal, abusive, and painfully frank—"intense" would be a good, but mild, way to describe him.

He hated God and openly cursed Him, in between cursing at me. I was really frightened to be around this guy. He would tell me "blood and guts" stories about Vietnam and would make threatening gestures toward me. I could think of lots of good reasons not to visit him anymore, but the Lord kept telling me, "You must go back to see him."

As I continued to visit this man, I realized that he was actually teaching me how to speak and how to listen. Ed told me at the outset that if I wanted to continue to visit him I would have to conform to certain communication guidelines. He pulled out a sheet and began to read them off. The Lord can and will use anyone and anything to accomplish His purposes. If God could speak through a donkey, can He not also speak through rough, unconverted humans? Ed is very intelligent, but it was humbling for me to admit that the Lord was teaching something through him.

One day while visiting with Ed, he related this story to me. He said that one of the times I had come to visit with him, he said to himself as he watched me walk up the sidewalk, "Here comes Christ's little ambassador. I'll just use this opportunity to get back at God for all the suffering and bloodshed I experienced in Vietnam." He blamed God, of course, for all the horrors of war.

His plan that particular day was to provoke me to anger in order to provide him an excuse to cut my throat. We were in his backyard that day, and he was trying to upset me with his abusive rhetoric, but his plan wasn't working. (Remember, I had been through years of that kind of verbal abuse already with my wife.)

He decided he would go ahead and cut my throat anyway. But when he went to reach for his knife, which was in his pocket, he told me he could not move his arms. My angel had a hold of them. He said he became very intimidated in my presence.

God used Ed to teach me certain things, but it is only the power of the Holy Spirit that can help us put godly principles into action. Speech is such a powerful tool that needs constant refinement by the Holy Spirit.

Just as we inhale and then exhale, so we must listen before we speak. Ecclesiastes 5:1, 2, in part, says, "Be more ready to hear, than to give the sacrifice of fools ... Be not rash with thy mouth." Proverbs 18:13 says, "He that answereth a matter before he heareth it, it is folly and shame unto him."

Moses, when he was instructed of God to go and speak to Pharaoh, distrusted his own ability to say the right words. And the Lord said to Moses, "Who hath made man's mouth?... Now therefore go, and I will be with thy mouth, and teach thee what thou shalt say" (Exod. 4:11, 12).

The word "teach" in verse twelve is the same Hebrew word translated "rain" in Hosea 6:3 where God says, "Than shall we know, if we follow on to know the Lord: his going forth is prepared as the morning; and he shall come unto us as the rain, as the latter and the former rain unto the earth."

Not one of us will ever receive the outpouring of the Holy Spirit in latter rain power while there remains one spot on our character. And how important is our speech in this process? Let the Lord tell us: "If any man offend not in word, the same is a perfect man, and able also to bridle the whole body" (James 3:2).

I have discovered that real union with the Father, Son, and Holy Spirit does not begin until we have this experience that James is talking about. There is a union with God that many professed Christians know nothing about because it does not begin until we overcome all of our sins. Fortunately, Jesus helps us all the way through this process until we reach ultimate union with Him, which is the fullness of Christ that fills us.

All of the facets of a relationship with Jesus—perfect conversation, abiding in Him and He in us, complete union with God, and complete brokenness of heart—are indissolubly linked together, and we must all in one way or another experience these if we are to "all come in the unity of the faith, and of the knowledge of the Son of God, unto a perfect man, unto the measure of the stature of the fulness of Christ" (Eph. 4:13).

The Spirit of Prophecy supports this idea. "We must war against temptations without and within. We must gain the victory over self, crucify the affections and lusts; and then begins the union of the soul with Christ.... After this union is formed, it can be preserved only by continual, earnest, painstaking effort" (*Testimonies for the Church*, vol. 5, p. 47).

If that statement did not make it clear, here is one that is even clearer: "Pride, selfishness, vanity, worldliness—sin in all its forms—must be overcome if we would enter into a union with Christ. The reason why many find the Christian life so deplorably hard, why they are so fickle, so variable, is that they try to attach themselves to Christ without first detaching themselves from these cherished idols" (*Ibid.*, p. 231).

When I first realized what these statements were saying, I had to re-think my whole Christian experience. If union with Christ begins when we overcome all known sin, I had never had a real union with the Father and Jesus. I do not mean to say that a person doesn't have a relationship with the Lord until they have this union. There are stages in a relationship. There are degrees of intimacy. But it is obvious as we read the Bible that there were certain people who enjoyed a very close union with God. I think of Moses, Abraham, Job, David, Daniel, Enoch, Elijah, John, Peter, and Paul. It is our job to determine how close a union we will have with Jesus, the Holy Spirit, and the Father. The potential is open-ended based on our response to the Lord's overtures. It all depends on what we will allow the Lord to accomplish in our heart. God is always one hundred percent committed to a relationship with us, but He can only get as close as we let Him.

It is in the glory of this union that God begins to show us all of our unknown sins and give us victory over them. The following statements from the Spirit of Prophecy taught me this truth: "As the branch must abide in the vine to obtain the vital sap which causes it to flourish, so those who love God and keep all His sayings must abide in His love.... All who are really in Christ will experience the benefit of this union.... This connection with Christ will result in the purification of the heart and in a circumspect life and faultless character" (*Testimonies for the Church,* vol. 4, p. 355).

"As Christ overcame every temptation which Satan brought against Him, so man is to overcome. And those who strive earnestly to overcome are brought into a oneness with Christ that the angels of heaven can never know" (*The SDA Bible Commentary,* vol. 7, p. 926.

"Justification means that the conscience, purged from dead works, is placed where it can receive the blessings of sanctification.... Sanctification means habitual communion with God" (*Ibid.,* p. 908).

The word communion in the Bible means, amongst other things, "intercourse." As it is with the physical, so it is with the spiritual. Through the consummation of the marriage relation in the blending of our spirit with the Holy Spirit, rebirth is the fruit of this union.

How can we know if this union is happening in our life? One way is explained in the following statement: "How little do we enter into sympathy with God on the point that should be the strongest bond of union with us and Him—compassion for depraved, guilty, suffering souls, dead in trespass and sins" (*Testimonies for the Church,* vol. 8, p. 31). How close of a bond do you want with God?

Testimonies for the Church, volume 6 states, "No one can be truly united with Christ, practicing His lessons, submitting to his yoke of restraint, without realizing

The Seven Thunders

that which he can never express in words." I completely understand this statement, because I cannot express to you what has happened inside of me. And if you have this experience you will not be able to completely explain it to others.

I encourage you to ask Jesus for this experience, this union. Only in asking do we receive. When I ask God for things, I always ask in the superlative sense. I say, "God, please give me a love for You and a love for souls more than anyone has ever known. Make me more sensitive and respectful of Your feelings than anyone has ever been. Make me more useful in Your vineyard than anyone has ever been."

What do you think God will do with prayers like that? Do you think He will ignore or deny them? Do you think God longs to hear prayers like that from His people? All of us should be praying for a closer walk with Him than anyone has ever had.

These are not selfish prayers if our heart is right with God. In fact, something ironic happens when we pray like this. It becomes our sole motive and responsibility, our highest joy to look at every soul we see and say within ourselves, "It is my highest duty to help them get to know Jesus even better than I do, and I'm asking to know Him better than anyone ever has."

Recently I read a statement that exemplifies and expounds upon everything that I'm trying to express here. It solidified and sealed up my desire for this union with Christ when God brought it to my attention. "With the great truth we have been privileged to receive, we should, and under the Holy Spirit's power, we could, become living channels of light. We could then approach the mercy-seat; and seeing the bow of promise, kneel with contrite hearts, and seek the kingdom of heaven with a spiritual violence that would bring its own reward. We would take it by force, as did Jacob. Then our message would be the power of God unto salvation. Our supplications would be full of earnestness, full of sense of our great need; and we would not be denied. The truth would be expressed by life and character, and by lips touched with the living coal from off God's altar. When this experience is ours, we shall be lifted out of our poor, cheap selves, that we have cherished so tenderly. We shall empty our hearts of the corroding power of selfishness, and shall be filled with praise and gratitude to God. We shall magnify the Lord, the God of all grace, who has magnified Christ. And He will reveal His power through us, making us as sharp sickles in the harvest-field" (*Sons and Daughters of God,* p. 30).

Now, let me share with you how God began to fulfill my desire for this special union with Him. One night I had just gotten to sleep when the phone rang. It was Ed. He said, "The bombs are going off in my head."

"What can I do? The only thing that I know how to do is pray. Would you like me to pray for you?" I asked.

He agreed to let me pray, so I prayed and then we hung up. I chuckled to myself saying, "This poor guy really has problems."

As I lay back down on my bed, my conscience smote me. Why didn't I feel more deeply for this man's torment, I wondered. I called out to God and said, "Lord, let me feel the love that You feel for this man. Let me feel the love that You feel for all sinners. Let me cry, Lord!"

Well, I thought maybe I would feel this warm fuzzy feeling in my heart or something. But I was not ready for what happened next. My stomach tied up in a knot, forcing all the air out of my diaphragm and out of my mouth. I started trembling uncontrollably. It was the most empty, dark, frightening feeling I've ever experienced. As these feelings engulfed me, I prayed in my head, *Turn it off, Lord. That's enough!* I don't know how long it lasted, but as it subsided I thought, *That couldn't have been from Jesus; that must have come from the devil.*

I said out loud, "Was that from you, Jesus?"

Jesus spoke to my mind and said, "I let you feel just a little bit of what I felt on the cross."

I have never been the same since that time. I look at people differently now. I don't want anyone to drink of the wine of the wrath of God. "Lord, let them have my place in Thy kingdom, if that were possible, so that they might be saved." I needed that experience in order to love the unlovable.

Ed was one of the unlovable people who God kept asking me to minister to. One evening Ed called up and asked me to come over. He had been drinking heavily before I arrived. He was telling me his troubles, and I tried to tell him about the great love of Jesus and how He suffered and died on the cross for our sins. He angrily retorted, "Don't tell me about that. I've seen a man skinned alive and then tied to a tree so the ants could finish him off. Don't tell me about suffering."

Ed pulled out a big knife. He asked me if I thought he could throw the knife and stick it within one inch of the doorknob of the kitchen door. I just shrugged my shoulders. He threw the knife a few feet away from the door and the knife stuck about a half inch from the doorknob. He retrieved the knife and continued throwing it, sticking it in various places on the door. He never missed once. He threw it backward while facing away from the door and stuck it. He even threw backward while walking and stuck the knife in the door. He was very drunk, and with each passing minute, he became more and more verbally abusive toward me. Then he barked out, "Why didn't you believe me that I could do what I said I could? What do I have to do to you to prove I am what I say I am?" Then he gestured with his hand an imaginary line across his chest and neck, insinuating that he was going to cut me with the knife.

He had a crazy, deadly look in his eyes. I just kept silent, praying for protection. I couldn't help thinking, "What if the angel doesn't hold his hands this time?"

Finally he calmed down, and a little later I left.

A day or two later he called me up and said, "Come over; I want to talk to you."

I said to the Lord, "Do I have to, Lord?"

I knew that if I refused or made an excuse Ed would mock my God, so I went.

He was drunk again, and after a few minutes of my arrival, he pulled out his big knife again. He started throwing it across the room and sticking it in the wall this time. This night, as on the previous night, he became very angry and started threatening me again, making motions with his hand about what he wanted to do to me with the knife. He had that crazy look in his eyes, and was saying, "What do I have to do to you?"

I was claiming God's promises, but my heart was pounding. I thought about bolting for the door, but I knew he could hit me on a dead run with that knife. Besides that, how would that make Jesus look if I were to show any fear? I just kept my gaze downward and prayed silently. Finally he calmed down, and I was able to get out of there.

A couple of days later he called me up and said, "Come on over. I want to talk to you."

I said to the Lord, "Do I have to, Lord?" I really thought that this guy was going to kill me, but I decided that if my life were to be sacrificed in this way for Jesus, I would do it.

When I got to Ed's house, he was drunk as usual. After a few minutes he pulled out that big knife. He walked right over and handed it to me, saying, "I want you to have this. There will be no more demonstrations of this sort anymore. You've passed the test. You're a brave man."

He asked me later why I wasn't afraid of him. I was very much afraid of him, but Jesus isn't afraid of anyone. I chose the courage of Jesus over my own fear. I sought the Lord's guidance on how to answer Ed's question, and the Lord impressed me to tell Ed that I wasn't afraid of him because I loved him.

Ed does not curse God anymore. He reads the Bible and prays. Although he has not made a full surrender to God, I believe the Lord is still working on his heart. When I spoke with Ed a few months back, he said, "Curt, I just want you to know that I'm alive today because of you." Of course, I know that it's really because of Jesus.

Several years have gone by now since I had these experiences with Ed. God has preserved his life for some purpose. He has survived a second-story fall, which dislocated his shoulder and cracked his skull; a car wreck that involved the car rolling

First Steps to Making Things Right

over about seven times; and seventeen stab wounds. Although Ed has delved back into drinking heavily after overhearing two church members making fun of some guests, Gordon, a member of our church, regularly visits Ed.

Gordon was the first person who spoke to me when I visited the Seventh-day Adventist church in town twenty plus years ago. It was at Gordon's upholstery shop that I used to pick up truth-filled tracts off of an inconspicuous wire rack years before I'd ever heard of the name Seventh-day Adventist.

When Gordon starts talking to Ed about Jesus, Ed gets up and goes outside. Ed is plagued with tremendous feelings of guilt. If only he would accept Christ's forgiveness, he could be free and at peace from the torture and condemnation of guilt he suffers, which drives him to drink and punish himself. Ed once got in my face and said, "Look in these eyes. This is the look of someone who has killed several people." It is true that I saw only darkness and pain in those eyes. I long to see the light and life of Jesus in those eyes. I beg the Lord frequently not to let Ed die before he lets Jesus inside his heart.

Like Moses, I needed a "fitting up" time before God could use me to lead souls to Him. And like David, in the Bible, I needed to be tested. God used Ed to teach me certain things, and He, in turn, used me to minister to Ed's needs. Now God brought another man into my life by the name of Ned.

His friends and enemies called him "Terrible Ned" because nobody could kill him, though many had tried. I gave him a new nickname: "Terrific Ned."

I met Ned at church. He would occasionally come with his mom, but soon after our meeting, he went to visit his father in California. His father is the president of a Harley Davidson motorcycle gang in California called *Los Vorachos*, which means "the drunkards."

After spending some time with his dad, Ned ended up in Las Vegas, where he hooked up with an outlaw motorcycle gang who lived in the desert practicing witchcraft and manufacturing drugs. They were in competition with the police for the drug trade. According to Ned it involved even judges. They would often get into shoot-outs with the cops.

Seven years went by before I saw Ned again. When I did see him, he told me, "I've been shot twelve times since the last time you saw me." Then he added, "You and me need to get together and talk sometime."

The next time I saw Ned he was walking down the street, so I pulled over and offered him a ride. He told me he had $30,000 worth of stolen jewels in his pocket. What he didn't tell me until later was that he also had an eighth of an ounce of heroin on him. He climbed in, and I let him off at a house where he thought he could sell the jewels. As he got out of the car, he again said, "Me and you need to get together and talk sometime." I gave him my phone number.

I didn't see or hear from Ned for a couple of weeks after that. I later found out that he ended up trading the jewels for more heroin.

Then one day there was a message on my phone from Ned. The message simply said, "Me and you need to get together and talk some time." I called Ned back, and we agreed to meet the next day after work. When I got home the next day, Ned was waiting there for me. Although Ned was not adverse toward me as Ed was, God was testing me nevertheless. My test with Ned was "judge not, lest ye be judged."

The Lord arranged for me to have a severely stiff neck the day Ned came over. Ned could tell that my neck was bothering me. It just so happened that Ned had learned a form of martial arts where they dislocate their opponents' joints. Ned told me, "Since I know how to dislocate bones, I know how to put them back in place. You might say I'm a chiropractor." He offered to help alleviate the stiffness in my neck. He had me lie down, and he gave my head a twist.

"Half a pound more pressure, and I could break your neck," he said. He told me the story of how, while he was in prison, his "cellie" was giving him some trouble. The guy wouldn't shut up, so Ned went over and put his neck out of place. The guy lay there for two weeks before he finally apologized to Ned, at which point, Ned went over and put his spine back in place. As Ned and I talked, he told me much of the degradation he'd been involved in, and he showed me his battle scars.

"Here's the one where they shot me off my motorcycle," he said. There was a neat round scar, about the size of a quarter, where the cop's bullet had entered his chest, a half inch above his heart. He had a half-moon shaped scar on his shin where he had "kicked somebody's teeth in." One of his fingers was kind of crooked on the end. That was where the bullet had gone through as he had endeavored to block a gunshot at point-blank range.

In addition to the violence, Ned was addicted to heroin. An accident had nearly severed his body in two, and he was always in pain. The doctors wouldn't give him any pain medication, so he used heroin.

"I've gone down two times," he said, referring to the two times he had overdosed on drugs. His heart had stopped, but he was revived in the hospital. "The next time I go down will be the last," he said.

As we continued talking, Ned said, "I want to stop hurting people; I want to change my life." Ned was a member of the Irish mafia, and he had left Las Vegas because he was being pressured to carry out an assassination, which if he didn't do would mean his own demise.

"I don't know how I can help you, Ned," I said. "I don't know how to do anything except pray. Would you like me to pray with you?"

"Yes," he said.

We read some verses from Scripture, and I prayed, and then Ned prayed. He confessed his sins to God, asking for forgiveness and for a new heart. He started crying. His own response surprised him. "I haven't cried in over five years," he said.

Ned and I started meeting to study the Bible. For several days after that, all Ned would do is read his Bible and watch Three Angels Broadcasting Network on television. His mother told me he was also reading *The Desire of Ages* by Ellen G. White.

Then I didn't hear from Ned for a few days. It was about two weeks after Ned had given his heart to the Lord that I came home from work to hear a message on my answering machine from Ned's mother. It said, "Curt, I have some bad news ... they found Ned this morning dead of a drug overdose."

The question arises, "Will Ned be resurrected to meet Jesus in the air when He comes?" I don't know, but my prayer is that Ned's family will be there, and I want to be there to find out.

You see, Ned had fathered a child several years before he died. Dage is the boy's name. He has been adopted by Ned's mother and stepfather. Dage is being raised in a Christian home and has the nurture of a loving church family. He is a fine young man, very respectful.

Although I was thankful to God for these experiences with Ned and Ed, I was still praying that God would open the doors for me to minister to young people. I tried to make myself available by hanging out where a lot of young people were, but my efforts were fruitless and no doors seemed to open for me. Then one day God said, "Don't ask for a ministry for young people; ask Me if you can have a share in My ministry to young people." I shifted my focus, and shortly after that I was allowed to minister at the Grant County Youth Service Center.

As rewarding as that was to be able to witness to and counsel the young people at the center, my real desire was still to be chaplain at the Grant County Jail. I earnestly prayed and pleaded for this opportunity. Then one day during my mid-day break at work I was kneeling in the cab of my pickup, and I said, "Lord, I know that You are going to give me an entrance into that jail, but I just wish You would hurry up!"

The Lord answered right back, "That's right, but if you really believed that, you'd thank Me for having done it already."

I said, "OK, thank you, Lord."

When I got home from work that same day, there was a message on my answering

The Seven Thunders

machine. The chaplain of the jail wanted to see me. That evening he invited me to be a part of their jail ministry. It is another story altogether to tell you the things that God has done in the juvenile hall and jail.

Not too long after Ned's death, I had to say goodbye to someone else I cared about. My wife had been in a nursing home for about three years when she passed away.

After she'd been in the nursing home for about a year, she went into convulsions one night, and by the time the staff discovered her situation, she was nearly dead. They were able to treat her, but she lost the use of one arm and her ability to speak. We never knew when the seizures would strike after that. She suffered pitifully. Oh how I agonized with God to heal my wife. Then, after about three years she started having trouble swallowing, and she was in constant discomfort.

I began to pray that the Lord would heal her or let her rest. One day as I prayed by my wife's bedside, I prayed out loud for God to relieve my wife's suffering one way or the other. I said, "Amen." And my wife said, "Amen." Chills ran up and down my spine because that was the first clear word I had heard from my wife in more than two years.

A few days later when I came to visit my wife, the nurses said, "We're glad you're here. There's something wrong with your wife." She was in the dining room. When I approached her, she didn't recognize me. She did not look at me at all. She seemed to have lost all touch with the outside world. And yet she was seeing something because her eyes were focused upward and moving around. She had a beautiful smile on her face and was saying, "Oh! Oh! Oh!"

After that she never regained much of her awareness to outside stimulus. The following Friday evening I went in to visit her. She had a fever and seemed to be delirious. I leaned close to her ear and said, "Stephanie, are you trusting Jesus for your salvation?" Slowly she nodded her head up and down.

That was the last time I saw her alive. The next day, the blessed Sabbath, she passed to her rest. I received an emergency call while visiting inmates at the state penitentiary. I rushed back to the nursing home and walked into her room as they were taking her pulse for the last time. Then a nurse closed her eyelids. It was about 3:00 pm.

I had settled the matter in my own mind, a long time previously, that my wife had passed the point of no return as far as being capable of making an intelligent, complete surrender to the Lord. I really thought that she was eternally lost. Hadn't I witnessed her reject nearly everything that at one time she had agreed was sacred?

The Lord Jesus Christ rebuked my shallow concept of His love, compassion, and desire to save every soul. As I reflected on my wife's peculiar behavior in the dining room the week before she died, the Lord impressed me that my wife's suffering was the means of her salvation. 1 Corinthians 5:5 talks about the spirit being saved by the destruction of the flesh. Of course, I must wait for the resurrection to see if Stephanie accepted God's free gift of salvation, but it is my hope that she made things right with her Savior.

My friends, the heart of God is larger than we can ever imagine. I have tried to find flaws in God's love, but I cannot. His love amazes me.

Chapter 8

REACHING THOSE BEHIND BARS

I want to share some experiences I've had with people in and out of prison. The names have been changed to protect their identity.

The Holy Spirit is very active inside the penal institutions. Sadly, though, after fifteen years of involvement in ministering to inmates, I have yet to see more than a few continue to serve the Lord after their release. I'm sure there are many who stay true to God upon their release from the correctional systems, but I'm referring to the ones I know of.

Although working in the adult prison fulfilled my longing for adventure, because of the greater element of danger connected with it, I think I loved working with the juveniles more than in the adult jail and prison.

About a year after I'd been visiting juvie as we call the holding facility for juvenile offenders, a teenager was admitted for killing his teacher and two students and maiming another pupil for life with a hunting rifle. A highly intelligent boy, Larry had had no history of violence, but he was the victim of a broken home.

When I first heard about the shooting, I said to God, "Lord, I'd like to be the one to hold that young man's hands and lead him in the sinner's prayer of repentance!"

It was months before I was ever allowed to talk to Larry, but one day he was allowed to attend our group church service. I told the story of my own life of sin. I told the group that I had murdered more people than any of them. I asked Larry to read a scripture out loud from the Bible. He read, "Whosoever hateth his brother is a murderer: and ye know that no murderer hath eternal life abiding in him" (1 John 3:15). Everyone knew that Larry was a murderer. A hush hung over the group. I told them how God had changed my heart and now I loved everyone.

After I finished giving my testimony, I asked the group if they could accept a loving God like I had described. Several hands went up indicating their favor. I looked back to where Larry was sitting next to his father who was there for a visit. His father had his hand up, but Larry was sitting with his head down. "Larry, what about you?" I asked.

He looked up and, trying to avoid the question, said, "What?"

Reaching Those Behind Bars

I repeated my question. "Could you accept a God like the one I described?"

There was a hesitation, then slowly his hand went up as he nodded his head. At that moment, Larry did not make Jesus Christ his personal Savior. He did not ask for his sins to be forgiven or for Jesus to come into his heart. But it was the beginning of a process that only God can disclose with accuracy. Larry and I became friends, and we enjoyed many nice visits together. I got to know both of his parents as well.

Larry had many questions about life and about God. I asked him if he wanted to ask God to forgive him of his sins, but he said he wasn't ready to do that yet. He said he wanted to know more about God first.

Larry was a delightful boy when he wasn't in a somber mood. The irony of the whole episode still baffles me. One of the guards told me that Larry was the most polite young man you would want to meet. I was caught up in the fervor with most everyone else who was seeking answers as to why such a nice young man would do such a thing, so I told Larry of my desire to know the motive behind his actions. He said, "I've never told anyone that except my parents and my lawyer." I let the matter rest, but God, in His kind and unusual way, rewarded me with the answer to my curiosity.

One night I had been visiting prisoners at the jail about a mile from the juvenile facility. It was about 9:00 pm when I went out to start my car, but my car wouldn't start. I decided to hitchhike home, which was about fourteen miles away, and retrieve my car the next day. I got to the highway that led home and stood under a streetlight to improve my chances of getting a ride at that time of night. I waited and waited. I think it was past ten o'clock, and I was beginning to despair when a little red car that sped past me suddenly pulled over and stopped. I ran up to the car and discovered that it was Larry's mother. She had just finished visiting with Larry and was returning home. We had a nice chat, during which I mentioned to her that Larry wouldn't tell me why he had killed those people. "He thought he was avenging evil," she said.

It came to pass that Larry was temporarily transferred from juvie to the adult jail. This was just before I was made a chaplain at the jail. I went to visit Larry at the jail, but we had to talk over the phones on either side of the glass partition. He'd been in the jail only about three or four days, but I noticed something different about him, and I said so to his face.

"I did it," he said.

"You did what?" I asked him.

"I asked Jesus into my heart," he said.

"When? How?" I asked.

"The other minister came to see me two days ago and offered me the gift, and I accepted it. And guess what?" he continued. "It's just like you said it would be; my cell is like a palace!"

I was so happy for him! Now I had another brother in Christ with whom to spend eternity. I couldn't help feeling a little bit let down at not being the one to lead him in the sinner's prayer of repentance, but I pushed those selfish feelings aside.

One day after Larry had been transferred back to juvie he requested to speak privately with me. He looked haggard and said he hadn't been sleeping well. He went on to say that he understood that God forgave him of his sins but that he was still feeling terrible remorse and guilt. He said that he just couldn't forgive himself. I explained that it wasn't up to him to forgive himself. I told him that God is his Savior, not him. I said that God takes away the condemnation, but we should always feel remorseful for our past sins. It was obvious that he wasn't experiencing the joy of his sins forgiven, so I offered to pray with him for forgiveness and to ask Jesus into his heart. We knelt down, and I held his hands as we prayed. Larry received life and freedom in the divine Son of God, and the Lord answered my request after all.

One day as I was talking to Larry I shared with him how I had suffered many years in an unhappy marriage. To give him an example of what I experienced on a daily basis, I repeated some of the vulgar language that my wife used to hurl at me. That night the Holy Spirit convicted me that I shouldn't have spoken those vulgar words. The next time I saw Larry I told him I had been wrong for using that kind of language. He said, "I know. I prayed to God to forgive you." I mentally threw up my hands and thought, *OK, I give up, Lord. Now I've got a little murderer praying for my soul!*

I attended one of Larry's court hearings and felt the combined disgust of the people who were gathered. There seemed to be no compassion for the perpetrator, himself a victim of a society gone mad through the rejection of God's moral law.

Larry was sentenced to life in prison and transferred hundreds of miles away, but that didn't stop me from making the five-hour trip to see him. I surprised him with my visit, and he said, "I can't believe you're really here!" I'm grateful to God for helping me to love Larry as He does. But if it had been one of my family he murdered, would I still be able to embrace him and tell him that I love him? That type of response is a demonstration of true love.

A year or so later our county was shaken by another grisly murder. Four teenagers had conspired to rob an elderly couple's home and steal their guns in order to use them in another crime. But the old couple awoke while two of the boys were still in the house. Another boy watched through the window. The girl involved in the crime was not at the scene when the murders took place. Under the influence of drugs, the two boys filled the bodies of the 89-year-old couple with scores of bullets.

When I first visited with Joe, who was housed at the adult jail, it was only three or four days after the murder. He described for me in great detail what had transpired. His bottom lip quivered as he spoke. He was badly shaken from the whole ordeal. They, or at least he, hadn't intended to kill anyone. They had taken a combination of potent drugs before breaking into the couple's house, and although this doesn't lessen their guilt, it demonstrates the danger of giving one's mind over to the control of Satan through the effect of mind-altering drugs.

I didn't waste any time in sharing with Joe the gospel message. I was delighted to find that he was open and already thinking about his standing before God. At the end of our conversation, we knelt down, and Joe received the God of the universe into his humbled heart.

Joe started Bible studies, and our visits became very special. Joe was in a cell alone for our first few visits together, and he commented that he felt a godly presence as we talked and prayed. Later they moved him to a tank with many other prisoners, and our visits lost the intimacy that the private ones had afforded. During one of our visits, I gave him a copy of *The Desire of Ages*, and he stayed up all night long to read it.

I became acquainted with all four of the youths involved in this murder, but I developed a closer relationship with Joe than I did with the others.

Ronald was the most obstinate of the four. He had fired most of the rounds into the old couple. He was sentenced to 72 years in prison for his part in the crime. We had some good talks, but he didn't have much use for God. He went on to be a troublemaker in prison, which resulted in separation from the other prisoners.

Mike, the other boy, seemed to be more of a follower than the others. He actually knew the old couple—he had worked for them and eaten at their table. His family sacrificed to pay for a good lawyer at a cost of $72,000, and he got off with a twenty-year sentence. I found Mike to be repentant and mild-mannered, but he stuck tenaciously to his family religion of Mormonism. In prison he was beaten severely and required hospitalization.

The girl, Janie, was quite a character. She was one tough little gal for her young age. Since she was only involved in plotting the robbery, she received the lightest sentence of ten years behind bars.

She was reluctant to show a weak side, but she confessed that she believed in God, although she wasn't ready to make any commitment to Him. In letters I received from her after she left for the "big house," she told me of her desire to start Bible studies with other ladies in her section. For some reason this was forbidden, so she led a one-woman protest. One day she somehow broke free from her escort and ran into a meeting room at the prison that happened to be filled with department of corrections officials for the state. She interrupted their meeting by going straight to the front of the room and confronting them with her concerns about being deprived of things such as Bible studies with other inmates. This action on her part caused considerable embarrassment for the prison officials and cost Janie dearly. They punished her by taking away the time she had accrued for good behavior, which would have possibly reduced her sentence. She told me, though, that they were soon allowed to have Bible studies together. In a letter not long after this incident, she told me that she wasn't very interested in living for God. She decided that she needed to stay tough in order not to be taken advantage of in prison.

Some prison settings are easier than others to develop and maintain a Christ-like walk. But it is difficult and challenging no matter how one views it.

Prisoners, in general, go through tremendous mood swings. One day they are on fire for God, and the next they may want nothing to do with Him. Many prisoners have the mistaken notion that because they have given their heart to Christ, in a short time the Lord will cause their sentence to be commuted and they will be liberated to serve God on the "outside." On occasion this has happened, but it is very rare. When some prisoners don't find themselves being released, or their legal appeals failing, their happiness for God's love turns to distrust, and they turn their back on Him altogether.

This was the case with a man named Tom who had been given a long prison sentence for murder. He found in Jesus a Savior and Friend while he was in prison. He had a strong testimony and was very influential with some of the other inmates, one of whom directed me to him. Tom and I became fast friends. We had some good visits and began corresponding by letters also. He had exceptional insight and wisdom of life in general and also in spiritual matters.

Then I met a man in a jail in another part of the state who was actually there when Tom had committed his crime. Though he hadn't actually seen it happen, he had been on the other side of the door of the bathroom when it happened, so he told me all the details.

One day, another chaplain and I were visiting Tom, who was on the other side of the bars in his cell. We asked to have prayer with him, and he agreed. We knelt in the walkway with our legs extending behind us. An inmate coming along the walkway had to step over our legs to get by. I hadn't paid any attention to this, but after we got up, Tom said, "That was a real witness."

"What do you mean?" we asked. Tom went on to tell us that the man who had stepped over us was a Muslim. He said that the Muslim chaplains don't come out to the cells to visit their brothers of the Muslim faith. In fact, he told us that the only religion that had chaplains that came out to the cells were Christians.

I watched over the months as Tom turned away from God, then back to Him, and then away again. One time he wrote to me and said that if I came to see him not to talk about God. Tom became unmanageable and was moved to a prison within a prison, solitary confinement, or "the hole" as it is known on the inside.

I went to see him once in "the hole," but he either didn't recognize me or didn't want to be bothered. He put his pillow over his head and went back to his pitiful pastime of sleeping even though it was midday.

On the other hand, there are converts among convicts who seem to have an indomitable spirit of faith. Whether they had an indomitable spirit before they knew Christ or gained it afterwards as a result of faith, it's hard to tell.

One such prisoner was Wade. As far as I know, Wade was given a life sentence. I presume it was for murder. (It's not a good idea to ask about their crimes, but sometimes they offer the information themselves.) Wade has been a Seventh-day Adventist for some years. He'd been in prison about eighteen years when I got to know him. After Wade had been locked up for several years, he went in front of the review committee. His hope, like most lifers, is to someday win a parole. The committee liked his report and told him maybe he could make it in about fifteen more years. Wade said, "Praise the Lord!" Five years later he went before them again and they said, "Come back and see us in five years." He said, "Praise the Lord!" When Wade told me he had finally gotten his release date, he added, "Praise the Lord!" Wade is a Vietnam War veteran. After our government taught our young men to be killers, many of them returned to the States and worked out their frustrations just like they had in Vietnam—by violence.

Another Vietnam War veteran with a long prison sentence is Jim. He had been in prison for twenty-six years when I met him. Jim is also a baptized Seventh-day Adventist. His lungs don't work very well anymore after poisoning from Agent Orange, the chemical that was used to defoliate the jungle in Vietnam during the war. Jim's story of his conversion to follow Jesus Christ reminds me of the varied and intriguing ways that the Lord uses to reach people's hearts.

Jim was a genuine rebel. Finding himself in prison with a long sentence stretching out before him only inspired him to greater recklessness. He was branded a troublemaker with little hope of ever seeing the outside of prison. Jim had no use for God (if he thought there was one). It just so happened the heart of infinite love had His eye on Jim. Jim spent a total of six years in solitary confinement. He was doing about a year in the "hole," as he related the story, when he had some tobacco smuggled in to him. His predicament, though, was that he needed some cigarette paper before he could enjoy his contraband. He relayed a message down the row of cells about his need, to see if one of the other prisoners could furnish his demand. A message was returned to him from a few cells away. The man told Jim that he didn't have any cigarette paper, but he had a Bible, the pages of which substituted excellently as rolling paper. Jim replied, "Send some promptly so I can get to smoking."

What Jim received was nearly the whole book of Job, minus the last part. Jim decided that he might as well know what he was smoking, so he started to read that book of Job. After reading about all of Job's troubles, Jim said that he felt more sorry for Job than he did for himself. Jim didn't know how Job's story ended, but he said he just knew that it had to be good. With that, Jim gave his heart and soul to God and became a Christian.

Some time after becoming a Christian, and then a Seventh-day Adventist Christian through the loving ministry of a compassionate SDA nurse, Jim was actually given a release date from prison.

Jim was coming regularly to our Bible study/prayer meetings, but then he was absent, and I wondered why. The pastor wrote him a letter, and he showed up again at one of our meetings. After the meeting I asked him if I could visit him during the week, privately. He said yes, so I met him a couple of days later.

Jim told me that he had been praying for someone to talk to. He said that he didn't confide in the people at the institution. Jim was at a very low point spiritually because his counselor was very spiteful and found a way to have his parole cancelled. This counselor wouldn't even let Jim have any contact with his adoptive mother because Jim had been involved in a prison riot many years ago, where hostages had been taken by the prisoners. His adoptive mother was the nurse who had been instrumental in bringing him into the Adventist Church years ago. Now, because of this counselor, she wasn't allowed contact of any kind with Jim.

I was able to share with Jim about my own experience of suffering and disappointment and how it had brought me closer to the Savior. Jim and I had prayed together, and he was encouraged.

Jim was transferred to another institution shortly thereafter. I was able to see him there some time later, and his faith and courage were strong. His simple desire was to enjoy a little time out in the free world with his adoptive family before his lung disease crippled and killed him. Nevertheless, he has accepted the fact that he will probably be in prison until he dies or the Lord comes.

Jim is an enjoyable person. The Lord tamed the wild man in him, and I consider it a privilege to have associated with Jim in this life.

Stuart is another prisoner with an interesting story. He was convicted of a white-collar crime. His business partners didn't like the way he was operating and succeeded in getting an embezzlement conviction against him.

Stuart had considered himself a Christian for years but had used the knowledge of the Bible as leverage to elevate himself. He was a trained, Christian counselor, but he didn't have a personal, saving relationship with the Lord Jesus Christ. After he'd been in prison for some time, he became seriously ill and was hospitalized for about six months. They didn't think he would live.

While flat on his back, Stuart watched the Three Angels Broadcasting Network constantly. With the influence of that sacred programming, Stuart was led to give his heart and life to God. Though not a Seventh-day Adventist, Stuart is an admirable Christian. He was respected and looked up to by those who knew him well. His gentle demeanor was winsome.

One of the most colorful and frank persons I met in the prison was Andy. With Andy's stark frankness was a very personable quality that one couldn't help but be drawn to. Andy started coming to our meetings after being befriended by a Seventh-day Adventist prisoner who was responsible for getting Adventist meetings started at that prison. He did it through a simple letter to a local pastor.

Andy told us his story one day. He ran away from home while a preteen to escape from a miserable home life and abusive father. Andy had no real destination, but he ended up in Hollywood, California, with seven dollars to his name. He met a prostitute on a street corner who took him under her wing. He lived with her for some time. In that atmosphere, it wasn't long before Andy became a drug addict and got involved in making pornographic movies. Andy had been in prison six times for a total of fourteen years. The last time he was due to be sentenced, he was told he was going to get about ten years. He was assigned to a different judge just before his sentencing. The new judge gave him only three years but warned him that if he ever came before her again, he would never get out of prison.

While waiting for his sentencing, Andy was held in a county jail. It was there that Andy met his Savior, Jesus. Here's how Andy related the experience: It was well known by the authorities that Andy was an addicted drug user. They immediately put Andy in the "rubber room" upon his arrest. The "rubber room" is just that—all rubber. It is reserved for crazies and violent or self-destructive persons. Andy used to work out his frustrations by hitting himself in the face and other painful actions. Andy was going through drug withdrawals in the "rubber room" and was very sick and depressed.

Andy told us that God beat him up for thirty days while he was in the "rubber room." He said that the "rubber room" was filthy because it rarely ever got cleaned. They couldn't trust prisoners in the "rubber room" with cleaning implements. One day Andy was bent over the rubber toilet as if he were going to throw up. As he was peering down at the putrid, grotesque bowl, God spoke to him. Andy said God told him, "Do you see that filthy toilet? That's what your life looks like to Me." That was the last thing Andy could take. After being beat up mentally by God for many days, and now that denunciation, Andy was defeated. He surrendered his heart and life right then and there to God.

When Andy was coming to our meetings, it was obvious at times that he was still undergoing massive spiritual struggles. He was fighting a desperate battle against doubt and fear. It was obvious that God was dealing with Andy. He said that the Lord still had to beat him up frequently to keep him humble.

Andy refused to do formal Bible studies with anyone, yet he would come to our meetings and relate things that the Holy Spirit was teaching him. These teachings were right in line with the Seventh-day Adventist beliefs.

Andy had had contact with many different Christian groups over the years and had adopted a Christian attitude at times but had never known a real saving relationship with Christ until the "rubber room" experience. We were Andy's first contact with Seventh-day Adventists, but by this time in his life, Andy was skeptical and suspicious of all religious organizations and Christians in general. Andy told us that he had been promised many things, many times, by various Christian groups and individuals. They had disappointed him so many times that he couldn't bring himself to trust anyone anymore.

One day at the prison, Andy didn't show up for the meeting. This was unusual because prisoners don't have the option of being out-of-town at their leisure. We asked the other inmates who knew Andy as to where he was, and we were simply told that he had personal problems. Later that week I was at home when I happened to think about Andy. It was Wednesday evening, and I decided to write a letter to him. I called the pastor who I was going into the prison with to ask him for Andy's Department of Corrections number, so I could get a letter to him. The pastor was just on his way out of his house with his family to go to prayer meeting at church, when he heard the phone ring. If I hadn't talked to the pastor right then, I probably wouldn't have followed through with sending a letter to Andy.

I mailed the letter the next day, which was Thursday.

The following Monday Andy was present at our meeting. He was as talkative as ever and related this story to us: It seems that he had been giving in to discouragement. The reason he hadn't come to our meeting the week before was because he didn't believe that the Christian life really made a difference in helping people to truly love one another. He didn't feel loved and was ready to turn away completely from following God. Andy said that he told God that if He, God, didn't have just one person who claimed to be a Christian who cared enough about Andy to write a letter to him, he didn't want anything more to do with God. Andy said that as he said that to God, he threw his Bible aside. He had never received a personal letter from any of the Christians who had supposedly befriended him over the years.

As you may have guessed, my letter to Andy arrived within a day of this episode. Andy's heart was melted as he realized the far-reaching ways of God and His intimate love and care for His children.

Andy and the last prisoner I talked about, Stuart, were friends in the prison. One day they came to the meeting with something exciting to tell us. They had been together out of doors one day the previous week and were remarking to each other about how drab everything in prison was. There were some normally colorful birds somewhere near them. They said that even the birds appeared to be dull and drab. Andy and Stuart were awed by the personal, tender concern of their heavenly Father, when a few moments later they looked up to see the most beautiful rainbow, which seemed to span almost perfectly over the prison complex.

Andy seemed to accept us and our denomination more and more, but he was transferred to a work-release facility before there was time for him to prepare for baptism.

The pastor and I went to visit Andy at the work-release facility, and I went once by myself. Andy and I were allowed to leave the facility together for several hours. He took me for a tour of his old "stomping grounds." He showed me an area of about ten square blocks where he spent many years hardly straying outside of that area except when he was in prison. We were driving along and Andy said, "See that shop on the corner and the big window in front? I threw a guy through that window once."

"Why did you do that?" I asked.

"He tried to cheat me," Andy said.

Andy and I went for a long walk through an arboretum. He said that in all his life near there he had never taken time to walk through and enjoy the natural beauty of the varied plants and trees God created. He told me how he would park at the edge of the arboretum and smoke crack cocaine. Then he would race away in his pickup because he thought there were authorities coming after him from out of the trees. After the drug and paranoia wore off, he would smoke some more and go through a similar experience. Such was the life of Andy for years.

I lost contact with Andy after his full release from prison. There are many more like Andy out there. The details of their lives differ, but basically, it's the same routine. Many of them welcome short jail and prison terms as a chance to "clean up" from the vicious drug habit for a while.

Spirit of Prophecy tells us that Jesus desires us to go into the big cities and "hunt for souls." It tells us that the angels will lead in this search. We are guaranteed that the Lord will protect us from becoming corrupted in these depraved surroundings. How can we make the gospel attractive enough to these lost souls so that they choose to break free from their enslavement before they end up with a long prison sentence?

I'm dissatisfied with it, but I've succumbed to the conclusion that the only way God can save some people is to keep them locked up in prison.

If I can persuade one person to abandon a life of drugs and violence for a life with Jesus, I will feel that my own life has had a purpose after all. God has placed me in the prison system to be a witness for Him and to share His love with people who may seem unlovable by others who can't look past their mistakes and crimes. I'm grateful and humbled that God has used me and will continue to do so to share the gospel with individuals behind bars.

Chapter 9

LETTING MY LIGHT SHINE CLOSE TO HOME

Not only have I watched men come to Christ in prison, but I have also seen some of my old friends from the neighborhood I grew up in turn their lives over to Christ. Unfortunately, many have chosen to continue in their ways of self-destruction and violence.

One man from my old neighborhood has his own church now in East Los Angeles where he helps drug addicts and gang members find a better life in Jesus Christ. Frank was from a very rough neighborhood. He was known for being very fast with a knife—hence his nickname of Fast Frank. Frank was a small time gangster; he liked to rob savings and loans businesses. One day he and his brother robbed a large bank. They made off with several thousand dollars, but the police staked out our neighborhood and caught Frank when a friend tried to smuggle him out in the trunk of a car.

One time Frank took several hundred dollars worth of heroin away from a friend of mine. In revenge my friend hired a hit man, but the hit man who was supposed to kill Frank just stole the down payment money from my friend. After Frank found out that a man he knew was hired to kill him, he shot a rifle at him one day from a little distance away. It was a warning well taken, and even though there was no real threat on Frank's life, he didn't take any chances on being misunderstood.

Frank was the main heroin supplier to our neighborhood for a long time. Some years after I became a Christian, I went back to my old neighborhood and told Frank that I was living for Christ now. He just gave me a mischievous looking grin. He was moving a lot of heroin at the time.

When I heard that Frank had been converted, I was very surprised. Who can ever guess who and how someone will respond to the Holy Spirit's overtures? I am awed at God's workings. Recently I was told that Frank is no longer a Christian. It seems, at least according to one of my friends, that Frank feigned becoming a Christian to sever his ties with the Mexican Mafia. Apparently, becoming a Christian is the only way one can withdraw membership from that organization and live to tell about it. After a big roundup and imprisonment of many of the top leaders of this group,

Frank felt free to discard his "Christian" identity. I'm told that now he is a biker and a troublemaker.

God can do some interesting things with us if we let Him use us as He wishes. I remember a time I was visiting my old neighborhood. I spent the night at my friend's house. Nearly everyone coming and going were drug addicts and had violent natures.

One of the men living at the house was Rick. He had lost his wife to another man, and he was bent on revenge. Rick had hired my friends to fire bomb the car of the man who had stolen his wife away from him.

Years earlier I had helped Rick steal an expensive piece of machinery. For my part he had paid me twenty dollars. After I became a Christian, I wrote a letter to him confessing my new faith and asking his forgiveness for my part in the theft.

It was about three o'clock in the morning when Rick came home from a nightclub with intentions to carry out the fire bombing plans. I was already up having my devotions. I was kneeling in prayer when I heard him come into the room where I was. He stood there for some time watching me. I continued praying. My Bible was open in front of me. He hadn't known I was in town, and I hadn't seen him for years, nor since he had received my letter of apology. I heard him go back into the other room where my other friends were preparing to go carry out their task for him. Then I heard him tell them, "The plan is off. In God we trust; in God we trust."

Later I had a chance to talk to Rick. God had been working on his heart, previously. We didn't talk about the cancelled plans, but I was glad I had been used to help spoil them. Perhaps someone was saved from going to prison or being hurt.

Many people from my old neighborhood have died prematurely and without Christ. But it is so good to hear when one of them joins the family of God. I think of another guy named Rick. He was the drug supplier for the neighborhood for a long time. He moved to Alaska to escape prosecution in California. But he got in some serious trouble in Alaska, and after being arrested, escaped from jail and made his way to the town I was living in at the time. He was there for about a month before they tracked him down. They sent two Alaska State Troopers to find him, knowing only that he flew into a specific town in Washington about a month previous.

Rick had already found a job washing dishes at a Denny's restaurant. In fact, he was working at the time the troopers arrived in town. The troopers were hungry after their long trip, and they slipped into Denny's for a meal before they resumed their search for Rick. Of course, the troopers only had to look up from their table, which they did, and there was their man. Rick was taken to the local jail, which he escaped from. He was desperate, knowing that he was facing a long prison sentence in Alaska, but they caught up with him once again and took him to Alaska.

It was shortly after he started his thirty-seven-year prison sentence that I became a Christian. I wrote to Rick a couple of times and encouraged him to put his trust in the Lord. Then one day I received a letter from him after he had been in prison for about a year. He told me that he had been contemplating suicide. He had read the Bible from cover to cover three or four times during that year. He said that it was either going to be suicide or Christ, because he could not handle the thought of thirty-seven years in prison. Fortunately, he chose Christ and experienced the joy of God's pure love washing over his soul.

After serving twenty-eight years in prison, Rick was released. He is now married and has a family. The ending is good, but while still in prison, he hit a rough period of time when he turned his back on Christ and got involved in drugs and fighting in prison. Fortunately, he recommitted himself to Christ in 1994, and he is now a free man.

It took a string of miracles, he believes, to get him released from prison, but God worked everything out. The local newspaper in Alaska actually wrote up an article on his life and mentioned that he holds the unofficial record for the number of escapes from custody.

He and the Lord have been partners for many years now, and he never misses an opportunity to express his gratitude to God for saving him from a life of sin. Praise God!

Chapter 10

FRIENDS LISTEN TO FRIENDS

One thing I have learned from working in jails and prisons is that I was unable to share about Christ with people without developing personal friendships with them.

I met this one inmate while he was in the local jail. It took awhile for us to become friends because Mike was a "tinder box" ready to burst into flames. In other words, he was ready to fight at the drop of a hat. Many other prisoners learned the hard way because they weren't careful what they said to Mike.

I first met Mike at one of the services in the jail. He and his brother were both there. Mike was in his early thirties and had already spent half of his life in prison. He had twenty-six felonies to his credit, most of them as a juvenile.

Mike was put in the "hole" for fighting. When I went to visit him there, that is when I was able to get close to his heart. I sat there for hours and listened to the pitiful story of his life. Most of the people I was able to get close to would probably not even stop to give me the time of day if I had met them on the street. But when people are alone with their conscience, there is a difference, albeit most of the time it is a temporary humility.

Mike told me about growing up with an abusive, alcoholic father, whom he grew to hate. Mike went to adult prison at a very young age. There he learned to fight. "I fear no man," he would tell me. It's ironic to hear this from some of these men, and then see them cry like a child at their predicament or when the Holy Spirit gets hold of their heart.

In one instance, no sooner had I walked into a man's cell, when he burst into tears.

It was mostly through Mike that I was able to make many connections in my understanding of the drug subculture in my town. Although at one time I was involved in it, my exposure to it was limited. Most of the people coming and going in the jail seemed to know each other. I was privy to information that was sensitive, personal, and sometimes potentially vital.

Like most hardcore drug addicts, Mike had contemplated ending and had attempted to end his miserable life. For a long period, Mike neither ate nor drank water—all he did was pump drugs into his body through a syringe. Because of this poor lifestyle choice, he damaged his urinary organs—his urine was black when he went to the bathroom—and developed colon cancer, which he had surgically removed.

Mike told me that one thing that really discouraged and depressed him was the greed and selfishness of the addicts who bought drugs from him. On one occasion the weight of the world was closing in on him, and he decided to end it all. He filled five syringes with heroin, and one by one, in front of a few onlookers who tried to dissuade him, he plunged them into his veins, during which time he decried to his amazed audience his abhorrence of their selfishness. Mike expected that that would be the end of his life, and it should have been, but amazingly, he survived the ordeal.

Mike confided in me many things, and as I spent time with him, he grew to trust me and the God I represented. How can one not get personally involved with those who they are trying to love into the arms of Jesus? Mike would tell me, "I love you, man. You're the only true friend I've got."

Mike began Bible studies through the mail with a Christian woman named Kit. She and her husband, Peter, were tireless workers for the Lord. Though on a very modest income, they never seemed to run short of funds for books for prisoners or gifts of money to help the families of prisoners. I would make the contacts and this godly woman would take care of giving Bible studies to the prisoners and/or their families. In addition, this couple would visit the inmates at the jail and prison and visit their families in their homes. While the work of this couple is noteworthy and commendable, it doesn't seem so unusual until one understands that Kit had given studies to at least fifty-five prisoners within about two to three years while confined to a wheelchair and blind. She had a helper whom she paid out of her own small income. These prisoners, when Peter and Kit befriended them, knew they were loved. I wish we had a hundred more people like Kit and Peter.

Mike began to share his new knowledge after he made Jesus Lord of his life. There was a period of time when Mike was in one of the tanks of the jail with about fifteen or twenty other men. Everyone in that tank was studying the Bible, mostly because of Mike's influence. The Holy Spirit was influencing all of the men in B tank. One time I walked into B tank, and the TV was blaring, and men were playing cards, making hand crafted items, or just talking. It was loud and bustling with activity. Mike saw me and shouted, "Hey guys, let's have a Bible study!" In what seemed like a matter of moments, everyone in that tank was gathered together, quiet, and with Bibles in hand. We had prayer and a Bible study. Mike had been telling the men about the Sabbath. After Mike was transferred to prison, the men asked me more about the Sabbath, so I studied with them and explained the Bible truth about the Sabbath. This upset the head chaplain, a Sundaykeeper, and resulted in my dismissal from the jail as a chaplain. Bible studies, though, never stopped in that facility because Kit continually had new requests as new inmates entered the jail.

Kit and I got involved with Mike to the point of going to his court appearances and writing letters to the judge, prosecutor, and newspaper on his behalf. I have seen and heard of God going "out on a limb" in a sense to show people, like prisoners, that He has a fatherly interest in their lives. We saw, I believe, the intervention of God when Mike's sentence was reduced by more than three years.

Mike has been in three prisons since I met him at the jail. His relationship with God has been up and down, and I pray for him every day.

Mike's girlfriend, Lonna, had a baby that Mike believes is his. We made strong efforts to win Lonna to Christ. She had lost her husband, children, home, and dignity to the ravages of heroin addiction.

One day Kit invited Lonna to receive Jesus as her personal Savior. She accepted the invitation and had a brief taste of freedom. There was a sparkle in her eyes when I saw her the next day. Unfortunately, she succumbed to the pressure of her carnal promptings and relapsed back into drug use. Finally she ended up in jail, and there, without the ready availability of the heroin, she began Bible studies with Kit.

While in jail Lonna wrote to Peter and Kit. One letter was dated a mere month before Lonna was scheduled to be released. In it she told how she had found in God a loving Savior and Friend. She expressed her anxious desire to begin her life anew with Jesus after she was released from jail. She was very happy.

Kit had arranged for Lonna to live with an Adventist family when she got out of jail.

A couple of days before she was released, Lonna had been transferred to a neighboring county jail to rectify a minor infraction. Needing a ride back to her home county on the evening of her release, Lonna caught a ride with an acquaintance who was released at the same time. They no sooner got to their final destination than they were on the hunt for some heroin. Lonna was found dead of a drug overdose the next morning.

We had a startling wake-up call from that tragedy. The devil is "playing for keeps." We should have been there waiting for Lonna as soon as she was released.

It seems that the authorities had given Lonna some drugs to help her sleep a few days before she was released. I was told they gave her methadone, a "synthetic narcotic" that is more potent than morphine. I leave you to draw your own conclusions as to the sad end of what could have been a happy one. Fortunately, God knows how to render perfect judgment. He can discern the fine line between human weakness and ignorance as contrasted with presumption, stubbornness, and rebellion. I'm glad that God is not like me, and I'm glad I'm not the judge of other people's motives.

Kit attended the memorial service for Lonna. Her "thoughtful" friends played a song called "China Doll," which is about a girl addicted to "China White" heroin.

Another friend of mine who struggles with drug addictions is a guy I will refer to as Drew. Before I became a Christian, I met Drew one evening in a bar. Drew politely introduced himself and informed me that he and the other fellow at the table were believers in Christ. At that time the fact that they were alcoholics and heroin addicts didn't seem to have any relevance to it. I told them that I was into self-awareness and karma.

"I'll tell you one thing," Drew said. "One day the sky is going to roll back like a scroll, and Jesus Christ is going to appear through the opening."

"Sure, that will just be one more illusion like the one we are in right now," I said.

I was so wrapped up in the ideas of Buddhism and eastern religions that I dismissed his statement. It wasn't until after I became a Seventh-Day Adventist that I realized the error of my thinking and began to pray for Drew.

Over the years I watched Drew go from bad to worse. Occasionally I would see his name in the newspaper because of an arrest for various things.

Drew knew I had become a Christian, but he never appeared interested in talking with me about it. Once he made a remark to me that indicated that my witness to him was actually doing more harm than good. He had asked me how I was doing, and I said, "Alright."

"Alright? You are a Christian; you should be doing great," he said.

I didn't have the joy of the Lord that I should have had. I hadn't learned how to have that joy, but I recently learned about the joy of the Lord, and I will share about that in a later chapter.

A little while later I was scheduled to speak for the first time at the weekly worship service at the jail. It was a Sunday morning, and as the prisoners filed into the meeting room, I saw Drew enter, walk to the front row, and sit down. As I spoke, I shared my testimony during which I could feel Drew glaring at me. It was as if his eyes were cutting right through me. After the service Drew said that he would like to speak with me. I met him later in his "tank," and we had a nice long talk. He confessed to me that at one time he had walked with Jesus in a saving relationship for several months, but he had lost it. Now he just couldn't seem to make that same commitment again, although he longed for it.

Drew got out of jail, and several months later I happened to see him in town. He was clearly high on heroin, but he wanted to chat, so we went into a restaurant to talk. He had a friend with him who claimed to be a Christian, and he told me he was trying to help Drew. When the other man went to the restroom, Drew told me that the man was schizophrenic. Indeed, there was something strange in their friendship. The other man seemed to kind of hover over Drew like a protective mother hen.

Later I found out in fuller detail from the other man how he had met Drew. It seems that Drew had been living in Spokane, but was not doing well—he was battling serious heroin addiction at the time. The other man was in his own apartment one evening during the winter when he felt impressed by the Holy Spirit to get in his van immediately and start driving. He did so, and as he drove, directions popped into his head as to how to proceed. He drove a hundred miles to Spokane and was directed to a large hospital. He was told to go into the hospital. In the lobby of the hospital he was told to go over to the telephones. On one of the telephones there was a man talking. He was told that he was to help that man on the phone. He went up to the man and said, "God sent me here to bring you back to the town where I live."

The man on the phone just happened to be Drew. Drew said, "I don't want to go with you, but you can give me a ride to where I'm staying." When they got to where Drew was staying, he got out of the van and started walking toward the door of his lodging. Just before he reached the door, he changed his mind and ran back to the van and accompanied the man to his hometown. The man found out about Drew's drug problem and made sincere efforts to help him, but it was in vain. Drew wasn't ready yet. What Drew gained from this episode in his life was that he was able to spend a few days with his mother before she died since she lived in the same town as the man who helped him.

It wasn't long before Drew ended up in prison. I had no idea which prison Drew was in as I had lost track of him. Months later I was at a prison preparing to conduct an Adventist service, and in walked Drew. We immediately started to chat. Drew said, "I finally did it."

"You finally did what?" I asked.

"I finally surrendered my whole life to Christ," he responded. He was nearly jumping up and down as he told me of his newfound joy. He told me he wanted to go to college to become a counselor or pastor—I don't remember which.

I have lost contact with Drew since he has been released from prison, but I'm sure God has plans for us to meet again in the future.

To me, relationships with others are my most precious assets in this world. Money has very little value to me except as an aid in building relationships with people. I've been taken advantage of, monetarily, many times by so-called "friends" and acquaintances. I look at it as an opportunity to forgive them, setting forth the example of my Savior, which they need to see.

When I left Los Angeles, I made a resolution that I would help my friends escape that life by paying their way up to Washington if they were inclined to come up. A friend of mine named Horace finally called me one day and said he'd like to come up for a visit. I made the mistake of sending him a money order instead of a bus ticket, and the $150 went into his veins in the form of heroin.

Fortunately, he did eventually come for a visit, and I was able to share with him some Bible truths that in his drugged out mind he has clung to ever since. He was raised a strict Catholic but no longer respects the Catholic or Sundaykeeping churches since he found out about the fourth commandment and the Sabbath.

When Horace left Washington to return to Los Angeles, he hitchhiked home. He said the second car that came by stopped and picked him up. The man took him all the way to his doorstep, about 1200 miles. Horace said the man even hung around for a couple of weeks. He said to me, "And guess what? He was a Seventy-Seven-Day Adventist." (Some of my friends aren't very intellectual. Horace graduated from high school, but he is illiterate and can't even fill out a job application by himself. Though illiterate, Horace has "street smarts.")

Horace died of a drug overdose not long ago. I just happened to be in Los Angeles at the time of his funeral. In attendance were many of my old friends from the neighborhood where I grew up. Little had changed in most of their lives. I was able to apologize to some of them for my past, and I passed out some copies of my life story to some of them.

I am thankful that God has allowed me to return to some of my former "drug buddies" and exert an influence toward liberation from their enslavement.

One case, for example, is Darren. He is the man who originally invited me to Washington. I feel partly responsible for the trouble he has had because it was at my prompting that he and I started using heroin. I had limited funds, so I didn't use drugs as heavily. Darren had much more money and went at it hard. After I became a Christian, Darren kept using drugs. One day shortly after I was converted, a mutual friend of Darren and I arrived in town wanting to see Darren. Upon not locating Darren, this man asked if I knew where he might be. I made a call and sure enough Darren was at the drug supplier's house. The drug supplier said, "He's out in the yard passed out."

The friend and I went straight over to see what was going on. When we got to the pusher's house, my friend went to attend to Darren, and I went in the house with the drug supplier, who I knew. "I heard you stopped using heroin," he said.

"That's right," I responded.

He proceeded to pour out a pile of China White heroin on the table. "Go ahead and fix yourself up." He insinuated that I could have a free dose.

"No, thanks. I don't want any," I stated.

He could not believe that I had the willpower to refuse. But I had something better inside me than the sensation of drugs. The devil still tempts me on this point, but I still have something better inside—Jesus!

Meanwhile, outside the house our friend was having difficulty reviving Darren. He was barely breathing. If we hadn't come when we did, Darren might have gone blind, or worse. As it was, one side of Darren's face was paralyzed, but he fully recovered after about a day.

Darren lost virtually everything he had to the expense of drugs, including a very good job. One day he approached me and asked if I could help him get off of the drugs. I told him the power was from God, not in counseling or programs and gimmicks. He said that he was desperate and would try God. We knelt down to pray, and I told him to repeat after me, since he was not accustomed to praying. This procedure was working fine until we came to the part where I said, "Please come into my heart, Jesus."

I could hear Darren struggling to say it, but the words literally would not come out of his mouth. Instead he said, "And please help me!" Needless to say, there was no deliverance from his drug habit that day or the near future.

After that Darren moved to the other side of the state, and I heard news that he was doing good, then bad, then good. I went to see him. His girlfriend had helped him, and he had actually taken Christ as his Savior. I could tell though that self had not died, and sure enough, it was only a matter of time before he relapsed back into his heroin addiction. Each time he seemed to get worse than before. I heard that he was using up to $250 per day of heroin. He would fill up eight syringes with heroin before he left for work in the morning, and every hour or so he would plunge one into his vein as he went about his work.

Recently, Darren called me after about ten years of no contact. He said that the last time he came off heroin he had to spend seven days in the hospital in the intensive care unit. It would have killed him otherwise. More recently I received a letter from Darren telling me that he has found in Jesus Christ an intimate, personal Savior and friend. I pray that that relationship will never be broken.

It is sad to live in a world full of suffering, pain, and sorrow. I have wept for and with many of the people I have written about. Yet at times I have laughed with them. It is a stark reality that many of the people we endeavor to help lead to the kingdom of heaven will not be there. I remember a Spirit of Prophecy statement I read one time that talked about doing good to people for the sake of doing good because what little enjoyment they find in this life is all they want and all that they may ever know.

Why aren't all Christians asking Jesus to let them feel His love for sinners? Prisoners are not all vicious criminals. I talked with a judge one time who sentenced some of the people I've been talking about. He said that if you were in a room full of people most criminals would appear and act just like anyone else. They aren't necessarily bad people, but they've made some bad choices.

Chapter 11

Helping Younger Offenders

One little boy I met in juvie makes me smile and sometimes chuckle as I think about him. He was only about 8 years old when I met him, but he was already a regular in juvie, having been in and out since he was 7. Lonny had an older brother that was a regular there, too. Sometimes they were there together. Lonny had a pitiful home life, and juvie was a substitute for the discipline, attention, and stability that he was missing at home. I met Lonny many times on the streets, and I would go looking for him at his home or neighborhood when he was not locked up in juvie.

But Lonny wasn't always happy about being in juvie, and sometimes he would break down and cry when I would walk into juvie and see him there again. Lonny's problem was that he had "sticky fingers"—he liked to steal things. One time, when Lonny was "in" again, I asked him why he was there. He didn't want to tell me, so one of the other children told me. "He stole a bicycle," one boy said.

"Why did you steal the bicycle, Lonny?" I asked.

"It was right there. What was I supposed to do?" he said, with apparent incredulity that I should question his integrity.

In spite of his problems, Lonny was such a likeable little guy. One summer I decided to take Lonny with me to an Adventist camp meeting up in the mountains. I got permission from his mother and his probation officer, and away we went. We had fun hiking and exploring in some old mines. At one point, Lonny slipped and started falling down the face of a steep rock on the side of the mountain. It wasn't a long way to fall, but he surely would have been hurt. Fortunately, another boy a little below Lonny reached out and caught him as he went sliding by.

Throughout the time at the camp meeting, it was a challenge to keep Lonny under control or even to keep track of him. He appeared one time carrying an item that he said he "just happened to find." I convinced him that we needed to return the item to the place where he "found" it.

On another day I saw Lonny going this way, then that way, and every which way on a nice bicycle. He said that someone had loaned it to him. Later that day some children came up to me and asked where the little boy who came with me was. I said I didn't know, but I asked them why they were looking for him. "He's got our bicycle," they said. They finally succeeded some time later of coaxing the bicycle away from Lonny.

Lonny wasn't interested in the planned, structured, activities for the young people at the camp meeting. These were too dull for this young man who was used to running the streets in search of adventure.

Although he did not attend many of the meetings, he encountered God in a simple prayer I prayed over him. On our first night in camp, Lonny and I made our way to our tent and crawled into our sleeping bags. Lonny immediately fell into a fit of coughing that carried on for about one hour without cessation. There was no way I could go to sleep with that noise, and I felt so sorry for poor little Lonny. I said to him, "Would you like me to pray about your cough?"

"OK," he said.

I prayed, "Dear Lord, please relieve Lonny from this coughing so he and I can get some sleep, in Jesus' name, amen."

Lonny coughed about three or four more times but then all of a sudden the coughing stopped, and I soon heard his slow, measured breathing. Lonny was fast asleep.

I hadn't heard Lonny cough during the day, and the next day I never noticed him coughing. But when we lay down to sleep the second night, the coughing immediately started again. After about ten minutes of this, Lonny spoke up, "Hey, Curt, can you pray for my cough?"

"Sure," I said. I prayed a simple prayer, thanking Jesus at the end.

Lonny said, "Thanks, Curt," and after a momentary pause, added, "Thanks, Jesus." He coughed about twice more and then was fast asleep.

Years later I found out that Lonny had ended up in a state penitentiary. Yet I believe that a seed of the gospel is in his soul that the Holy Spirit is tenderly watching over for the appointed time of germination.

****

One time I met a young man after speaking at the weekly service in the local jail. He was a nice looking young man, and he requested a private audience with me following the service. I said I would come to his tank later and visit with him. After making some other visits, I got around to his tank, and we began to talk.

He was not one of the "regulars" or one of the "locals." He was one of the many who get arrested on weekends, usually for drug possession. He was caught at a rock-

and-roll concert with two ounces of hallucinogenic or "magic" mushrooms that he had purchased from someone at the concert.

He didn't seem interested in spiritual advice, but he wanted some sort of legal advice, or perhaps he just needed someone to talk to. This young man was a sophomore in college. He came from a very proper home and was a respected officer of the college's student government. He was understandably worried about his family and friends at school learning about his arrest.

He felt that he had done absolutely nothing morally wrong. My attempts to present to him the offer of salvation in Christ were brushed aside. He knew it all, having been a theology major his freshman year. He did pay attention when I began to tell him of my own experience with drugs and how the Lord saved me out of that life. He had no rebuttal to my testimony and seemed thoughtful about it.

I asked him if there were many more young people who used drugs and listened to rock music at the Christian college he attended, and he said that there were. His answer didn't surprise me. I'd already heard similar stories from other sources about parties and such at this particular college campus.

****

Unrestrained sexual passion is eating the heart out of our society probably more than lying and theft. Many lives are ruined in many ways by this evil. I know a young man whom I'll identify as Kraig. I first met him when we worked together. It didn't take him long to realize that I was a Christian. He told me that his grandfather was a minister, and he invited me to come to meet him. Kraig lived with his grandparents. One day I went to visit Kraig and meet his grandfather. I also took a Bible study video, and Kraig and I watched it together.

Kraig told me much about his life. He shared with me that he liked to get drunk and fight. He liked to beat guys up in front of the girls so that the girls would admire him. Kraig told me that before he would go out to a party he would lie on the floor and implore the devil to enter into him so that he would be a fierce fighter. Kraig apparently got what he wanted because some time later I heard that he had fled to another state after putting a man's eye out in a fight.

Kraig returned to the area a year or so later after having trouble in the other state. It wasn't long until he was arrested, but not for fighting. By this time I was a chaplain at the county jail, and I made a special visit to Kraig's tank to talk to him. He confided a lot to me, but I had the impression that he wasn't telling me the whole story. He showed me the papers listing his charges, which were something like ten counts of child rape. It seemed that Kraig liked to find young girls at the parties who were obviously drunk. He would offer one of them a ride somewhere and then take her and force himself upon her. There were a few of these girls who testified to this at his trial.

Before Kraig's trial the prosecutor offered him a plea bargain. If Kraig would plead guilty to some of the charges or lesser charges, the court would sentence him to twenty-two months in prison. Kraig rejected their offer, maintaining his innocence. Kraig took his case to trial and was convicted on all counts. He was sentenced to thirty-seven years in prison. Kraig could have avoided this terrible devastation of his life if he had responded to my invitation to follow the Lord some years earlier. However, Kraig may yet make his peace with God. I saw him one time in the Seventh-day Adventist service in the prison. Since that time I have found out that Kraig has been released from prison and is a strong Christian, although not a Seventh-day Adventist. Apparently he got all but one of the convictions overturned.

Chapter 12

My Lord and My God

I have moved away from the prison work and I'm looking forward to a different kind of work for Jesus. My heart is sensitive to the men wasting away in prison. I am so thankful to God that this life is temporary, and they can receive eternal life right there behind bars. They can look forward to a better judgment if they love and follow the Lamb of God. I pray that they and I and you, dear reader, can one day receive a sentence with words like these: "Well done, good and faithful servant. I sentence you to eternal life!"

The more I seek to know God, the bigger He gets and the littler I get. Every day brings a new page, every year a new chapter to this story of my Lord and I.

My understanding of God's character is constantly being refined. It's like staring at a beautiful painting that keeps exuding richer and richer hues the longer you look at it.

This chapter is a testimony to the reliability of God as expressed through His unfailing promises. It is a testimony of God's love and His desire to give us the desires of our hearts.

There is basically only one way to increase faith, and that is to exercise it. There is basically only one proper way to exercise faith and that is to test God's promises. God gives us faith in increasing measure as a consequence of our successful use of the faith that we already possess.

My trust in God has grown as He has taught me to exercise faith in His promises.

As I stated earlier, one of the most important things in life to me are my relationships with people. I go out of my way to find out if I can trust people, and I have discovered that there are many ways to test a person to see if you can trust him or her.

A man and a woman pursuing a relationship toward marriage must establish a basis of trust in one another.

I've worked on the same principle in my relationship with God. I've tested God to see if I can trust Him. God has done the same with me. I found that I can trust God. That is what this chapter is about.

Psalm 18:30 says, "As for God, his way is perfect: the word of the Lord is tried: he is a buckler to all those that trust in him."

There is a saying that "a man is only as good as his word." I think the same thing applies to God—He is only as good as His Word. I have tested God's Word to see if I can trust Him. I've claimed His unfailing promises and found them to be true.

There were times when doubts and fears threatened to extinguish the barely smoldering fire of my faith, but I held on to God's promises, and my faith grew.

I didn't set out to test God's promises for the sake of increasing faith. I didn't set out to test God's promises to see if I could trust Him. I simply asked God if I could have a happy marriage after two miserable ones. I asked for a wife whom I could truly love and respect and vice versa.

I found out that God doesn't just give specific gifts to us at our every asking. To those who are in a conscious, deliberate, covenant relationship with God and are seeking to sanctify themselves and honor God, He works on a higher principle. Rather than simply giving for the sake of giving, God provides a host of valuable, spiritual assets that He knows we need.

I found out that among other things God will provide lessons preparatory to, and along with, the reception of the gift we desire. These lessons will not only help us heavenward but will condition us to appreciate the gift far more than we would have if He had simply given us the gift as soon as we asked for it. How I learned all of this is what I want to share with you. This is a most delightful chapter for me to write.

I remember as a young teenager dreaming about what I wanted when I reached adulthood. I imagined myself with a little home and a wife and children. I looked forward to a simple occupation from which I could return home to the loving arms of my family. As you already know, my life went far and wide of that mark. But God never forgets innocent childhood dreams. God wants us to be contented, fulfilled, and happy, even in this evil world.

In 1972 when I was about 17½ years old and my life was still a little less than totally out of control, an event took place thousands of miles away that I knew nothing about and was insignificant to most of the world. On May 14, 1972, a little girl was born. She was the second of two children and her parents adored her and her brother, who was a few years her senior.

Lana, as she was called, grew up to be a teenager with a rather normal life for a girl living in Eastern Europe. Her father was Hungarian, and she inherited his facial features more than her mothers'. They were subjects of the beast of communism, but the family learned to live with their circumstances, as did the people around them.

Unfortunately her father had problems and neglected his family. Lana's mother finally could take no more and divorced her husband. The security of a quiet and harmonious home was not to be for Lana. At a time when a girl needs the direction and support of both parents, she was deprived of this. The effects of the inharmonious and dysfunctional marriage of Lana's parents manifested itself in Lana—at the young age of 18, she entered into marriage with a young man who claimed to love her. She was seeking love and security, but she found out that her ill-advised marriage afforded her neither. Her husband made himself scarce for long periods of time and didn't respect her like she had hoped he would. Nevertheless, a beautiful daughter was born to them. Unfortunately, this girl too would not have the privilege of a loving home. Dana, as she was called, was an unwilling victim, as we all are in different ways, of the devastating results of sin, ignorance, and selfishness. Lana and her husband made a permanent separation in 1997 after about seven years of marriage.

When Lana was seventeen, communism lost its grip on her country in a brief revolution, and the country was catapulted out into the unfamiliar arena of the democratic free world and capitalism.

Lana was raised with the overshadowing influence of Orthodoxy, though it was superficial to her and to her family. Lana was lost and lonely in a world of hardships and disappointments.

Fast forward more than twenty years from Lana's birth. In 1995 Lana's brother was converted and became a Seventh-day Adventist. His attempts at witnessing to Lana seemed to have little effect, although she did at times attend church with him and his wife.

In August of 1999 Lana had a profound, peculiar dream. She dreamed that the world was soon coming to an end. There was an unfamiliar woman speaking to her in the dream and telling her these things. Apparently noticing her bewilderment and consternation, the woman in the dream told her that she must read Romans 8:14 in the Holy Bible.

When Lana awoke she remembered the dream and the text she was directed to. Lana was not at all acquainted with the books of the Bible, but she eventually succeeded in locating the passage. She read: "For as many as are led by the Spirit of God, they are the sons of God." Although the words didn't have a great impact upon her at that time, they produced a seed of the gospel in her heart. Lana called her brother Titi and told him about the dream. Titi and his wife, Lisa, invited Lana to come visit them in the town where they were living to talk about spiritual things. Lana boarded a train and headed to their town for the weekend. Afterward, she returned home and resumed her life as usual. Later, the woman Lana saw in her dream actually knocked on her door. She was selling truth-filled books door-to-door.

****

From adolescence onward I was the slave of my unrestrained drives for intoxication and pleasure. I abused my privileges and wasted my strength carousing at parties and such. The kind of wife I had dreamed about as a youth wouldn't have me, and I admit I wasn't worthy of a virtuous woman. Consequently, my first two marriages were unhappy failures. I know very well the age-old dictum, "You reap what you sow."

Nevertheless, when I did at last turn to the Lord and begin to serve Him, He began to prepare me for a great blessing. I have told you how God, in His wisdom, has persisted in refining the dross out of me—and the refining is still going on. God hadn't forgotten my childhood dream. God longs to give us the innocent things that will make us happy. Now I know this to be true, but then I didn't.

I never expected to have another chance for a happy marriage. I hadn't expected my second wife to die. I was prepared to ride out the storm to the bitter end. Also, I thought the world would end before now. I also held out a bittersweet hope that my wife would be healed. It was a sweet hope for her sake because of her pitiful suffering, but it was a bitter hope for me because of the relentless harassment I received from her.

After Stephanie died on November 9, 1996, I realized I was liberated from a yoke that had choked me for fourteen years. I had done what I thought was right to correct my past mistake. I stuck it out because of my love for God and my daughter, Spirit.

After a period of mourning and closure, I began to ask the Lord if it was really possible for me to have another wife.

I confided in some friends about my desire, and I was repulsed when one of them said, "Maybe the Lord wants you to remain unmarried like the apostle Paul."

I began to study the Bible and the Spirit of Prophecy about courtship and marriage. I read 1 Corinthians 7:7: "For I would that all men were even as I myself. But every man hath his proper gift of God, one after this manner, and another after that." I could not stand the thought of having to live alone or unmarried for the rest of my life. How I longed for intimacy and companionship with a woman who truly loved me!

I thought that the second part of that scripture must apply to me, "But every man has his proper gift of God." I really didn't know if God wanted me to have another wife. I had doubts as to if the Lord really wanted me to be happy that way in this life. I didn't think I was entitled to a happy marriage because of all of my past sins. I studied very carefully the second part of the passage. In the Greek "proper" means, "when they were alone." "Gift" in that passage comes from the Greek root word *charis*. I read the scripture back to God with these meanings inserted and claimed it as a promise—"But Curt Shearer has his, when they were alone, *charis* from God." I thanked God and asked Him for a sign that He truly was preparing to give me a loving wife.

A few days later I was visiting a Seventh-day Adventist church school. At Friday night vespers I saw a young woman who had been a student at the school but was now working there as a staff member. I was looking for help with the juvenile jail service and thought that this young woman might like to help with the music. I was also looking for a wife who would work with me in the jail and prisons. Although this young woman was many years my junior, I wasn't inhibited about that fact because I was looking for a young wife. I had read that Ellen White's son Willie married a woman about half his age, and Ellen White approved of it.

I asked this young woman if she would come and play her flute at the service that coming Sunday. I was surprised when she said yes. On Sunday we met and drove together to the jail for the service. The young woman's name happened to be similar to the word *charis* in the scripture that I claimed as a promise. She and I were alone when we drove to and from the service, and I believed that I had received the sign that I had asked of God—"when they were alone, *charis* from God"—for me to remarry. The problem was that I thought she was to be my wife based on this sign, and when I made known my intentions of wanting to court her, she carefully avoided me thereafter. I felt disappointed and dejected.

I didn't know how to go about finding the perfect mate, but I had read a book soon after my wife died about a young couple who had separately given their love life to God. They did not go out on dates to try to find their marriage partner. They waited upon God to reveal to them who their spouse would be, and God brought them together and blessed their commitment to Him by giving each other the perfect mate. So I gave the situation over to God. At the same time I realized that I had a part to play in the matter. I had to make myself available and also actively look for a wife. I had read the scripture in Proverbs 18:22 that says, "Whoso findeth a wife findeth a good thing, and obtaineth favour of the Lord." I claimed this promise and many others and set about in search of my wife.

I went to camp meetings, social gatherings, and meetings for single Adventists. I was rewarded with more disappointments. I thought, "This could take years, and I'm lonely now." I still thought that the world would end before I realized my dream.

I poured out my heart to God in despair, but I didn't experience much relief.

Then I met a man who had a beautiful young wife many years his junior. He told me to stop looking for a wife, and at the right time, I would receive one. He had been a bachelor for fourteen years and wasn't looking for a wife when this beautiful woman came into his life. Upon returning home after meeting this man, I saw no less than ten different rainbows in about the space of three hours. I wondered if God was trying to tell me something. I was confused. That man hadn't particularly wanted a wife, but I did. How could I not look for one?

One day while I was sitting outside, I saw a butterfly flit by. I wondered how that lonely little butterfly found a mate in the wide expanse of the open air. "Somehow God brings them together," I thought. Then I had the reassuring thought that just as the Lord finds a mate for the butterfly, so He would find a mate for me. I prayed many times for the Lord to help me find my "butterfly."

I had in my own mind an idea of what kind of wife I wanted. I told the Lord that, this time, I wanted a woman who had never been married. The Lord informed me that I wasn't going to get off that easy. He told me that He was going to give me a family. He reaffirmed that revelation to me in a couple of ways.

One time I was going to go into a prison many miles from home for the church service. I had been in that prison before, but this time the officials couldn't find my name on the current "call out sheet." There wasn't anything I could do, but rather than head home, I decided to attend a children's program at the local Seventh-day Adventist church. I had never had much interest in the children's programs at church, but as I watched these children perform, the thought came into my mind, "You had better get used to this."

Later, the Lord added to this experience by leading me to a scripture and impressing it upon my conscience. "Yet setteth he the poor on high from affliction, and maketh him families like a flock" (Ps. 107:41). Unfortunately, through lack of faith and trust, I endeavored to start relationships with women who had never married and had no children. These relationships were destined for failure, yet the Lord used each one to teach me an important lesson and prepare me for the special woman He was preparing for me.

As part of my effort, I joined an Adventist singles' writing club, where you get a catalog with pictures, descriptions, addresses, etc. I wrote to many women but only received a few answers. Every one of them turned out to be a disappointment. I was beginning to think that perhaps I would never find a wife who suited me. I wondered if it was all of my own devising when I thought the Lord had answered me.

I began to question God's love for me. Oh sure, I knew that Jesus' death on the cross was incontrovertible proof of God's love for me, but I found grounds for complaint against God because of my current predicament. At the same time, I couldn't help wondering if I was delaying the answer to my request for a wife by doubting God's tender concern for my present happiness. I wasn't experiencing joy, and it was obvious to the people around me.

I claimed Psalm 37:3-5 as a promise, asking God to give me the desires of my heart as it states in verse four. One day the Lord remonstrated with me. He told me that I wanted Him to fulfill His part of the promise, but I didn't want to fulfill my part—the condition upon which the promise is to be granted. It says, "Delight thyself also in the Lord." I wasn't doing that. I admitted it and asked God to help me. For some reason, though, I just wasn't able to delight myself in the Lord. I tried, but I wasn't finding that joy of the Lord. Nevertheless, I thought I was delighting in the Lord, at least for momentary flashes, so I continued to claim and trust His promises.

Then I received a letter from a woman in Eastern Europe. She wanted to correspond with me. In fact, in the second letter I received from her, she invited me to come visit her. I didn't know much about her country. I had no idea where it was geographically, except that it was in Eastern Europe somewhere.

I called my parents on the phone and told them I was planning to take a trip to Eastern Europe to meet a woman who I hoped would someday be my wife. Two days later my mother called me back and said, "Curt, the Lord said to me that the woman who wrote to you is not the one."

"What do you mean?" I asked.

"She's not going to be your wife. It's going to be someone who has had a lot of trouble like you … perhaps with drugs or prison," she added.

I thanked my mother for the message, but I didn't believe it. I had had two wives already who had lived loose lives like me. This time I wanted a virtuous woman. I continued with my plans to meet the woman, Brenda, in her home country by purchasing tickets for a flight in May. It was about mid-April, 1998. I called Brenda to let her know I was coming. I also wrote another letter to her just before I bought the tickets. The letters to and from that country usually took at least ten days to arrive and more often fourteen days. A few days after I bought the tickets, I received a letter from Brenda. She had changed her mind and didn't want to meet me after all. I had prayed that the Lord would make it clear if Brenda was the one for me or not. Her letter came to me in exactly six days.

I was let down again. Not only that, but the tickets were non-refundable. I tried to sell them, but with no avail. I said to the Lord, "I guess I'm going to take a vacation to Eastern Europe."

On the flight over there, I felt very low. I didn't really care if the plane crashed or not. I hated being without a mate so much that death seemed a sweet release from the pain of loneliness. I was distracted for a while from my spiritual stupor by talking to a beautiful Swiss woman sitting next to me. I poured out my whole life story to her and gave her a *Steps to Christ* to read.

I had contacted a man named Eugen by e-mail before leaving, and he was going to pick me up at the airport and give me a place to stay. He and his wife, Julia, were very kind and hospitable. They offered to help me meet some women, too.

One of the highlights of my visit was being able to speak in a juvenile prison to about 300 inmates. They were very receptive and friendly to me.

With only about four days left of my stay I met a woman who caught my fancy. She was a Seventh-day Adventist, so I trusted that we must be compatible. We wrote back and forth after I returned home, and then I made another trip there in December of 1998 to get to know her better. We decided to get married that coming summer.

I went back again at the end of April, 1999, with every intention of getting married to this woman. She had some serious emotional and mental problems, but I tried to overlook them. I believed that I had been prepared to handle her problems by what I had been through with my second wife. I was that desperate for companionship. The woman told me she loved me, and I thought I loved her.

She and I met with her pastor in order to counsel for marriage. The pastor said that we had to wait a few months to get to know each other better. I couldn't understand why he would say that. He said, "We pastors speak for God." To me his statement was the height of arrogance.

My fiancé decided to listen to the pastor, and she postponed our wedding to some obscure time in the future.

The Lord had instructed me never to condemn, criticize, scold, or lecture my prospective wife. I had endeavored to adhere to that rule, but this was too much for me to bear. I spoke in an agitated manner to her about her being so irresolute. She started to mock me, saying, "You're upset; you're upset."

I went back and told Eugen what had transpired. He said, "The pastor is trying to protect you."

"What do you mean?" I asked.

"Curt, this woman is not good for you," he said.

Also, my other friends who had observed her told me the same thing. I reviewed my experience with this woman, and it was unavoidably clear that she didn't have any respect for me. She no doubt had other motives than love for me.

My feelings for this woman were overpowering. I was willing to accept abuse and disrespect from her for what little affection I could get in-between times. I know now that it was not love that I had for her but infatuation. She was young and pleasant looking, and I was flattered by her apparent interest in me.

I went to the Lord to ask Him what I should do. I knew that my friends were right in their evaluation of the situation, but I couldn't find the resolve to end this relationship. Eugen had been frank and faithful when he challenged me with this question, "What's wrong, don't you trust God to find you another woman better suited for you?" I was without a rebuttal to that one.

The Lord led me to a scripture for my answer as He has done so often. Proverbs 15:22 will be forever stamped on my memory because it was more than just an answer to my question of whether or not to break up with my fiancé. The scripture says, "Without counsel purposes are disappointed: but in the multitude of counsellors they are established." I was faced with one of the hardest struggles of my life. I had to deny my feelings and respond to reason. I know now that I needed to get control of my emotions before God could give me a precious woman to share my life with. This is essential for an optimal marriage relationship.

I was having some health problems at that time and had embarked on a five day fast. Three days into the fast Eugen took me to my fiancé's house and almost forced me to break up with her. I announced to her that our relationship was finished. Ordinarily I was an emotional wreck around her, but the fast allowed me to transcend my emotions and do the reasonable thing with confidence and firmness.

God had taught me that reason must control feelings and not the other way around. He also taught me to respect His ministers and my brothers in the church. God later reconfirmed this lesson to me.

I had committed to friends and my church to spend a year in that country. I decided to stay despite my marriage plans falling through.

My friends in Eastern Europe took it upon themselves to help me meet other ladies. They introduced me to a nice woman who had never been married but wanted to be. We met together a few times, but after I gave her some flowers, she said she didn't want to pursue a relationship with me anymore.

It was like kicking a guy when he is down. I had had enough rejection for one lifetime. I took my complaint to God. My friends were questioning my experience and my testimony of God, and I didn't like it. I was not reflecting the joyful experience of a saving relationship with Christ, and it was obvious. Was my joy based on earthly contentment or in a loving God?

I went to the Lord for help. "Please teach me how to be joyful in spite of my disappointments," I pled.

About that time a man came to the town where I was staying to have a book printed at the printing house where I was working. I consented to put him up in my apartment for a few days. The man was handicapped but spoke almost constantly about how much he loved God and God loved him. He was truly joyful from deep in his soul, and it showed. I was rebuked in my soul because of my incessant self-pity and complaining attitude.

Right at that time Mark Finley of *It Is Written* ministries was holding evangelistic meetings in the capital city. They were broadcasting via satellite to all of the churches in that country and all over Eastern Europe. I went to one of the meetings and was invited to go backstage and meet some of the workers. In a little break room was a man reading a Bible. I learned later that he was one of the piano players who played on stage for the special music selections. I noticed also at later meetings that he never turned his face toward the cameras. When I saw him in that little room, I knew why. His face was severely disfigured. He greeted me and then began a beautiful, joyful testimony about how happy he was in Jesus Christ. I made a mental note of this just as I had with the handicapped man who was staying with me.

It was around that same time that I was obliged to leave the country and return again in order to renew my passport visa. I took a bus to Athens, Greece.

At the border as we were returning home, the border police asked to see my passport. In the picture I had a beard, but now I was clean-shaven. The police officer eyed me suspiciously. "This isn't you," he said. He threw a volley of questions at me, which I could hardly understand. He was clearly upset. A girl on the bus attempted to translate for me. He told her to shut up. They ordered me into the border guard office. Five of them stood looking at me and then at the picture and then at me again. "This isn't you," they chorused.

"Yes, it is," I said.

"No, it isn't," they said. We stood deadlocked. I was afraid that my stay in Eastern Europe was going to be interrupted or ended entirely.

What is this all about, Lord, I wondered to myself.

Finally one of the guards barked at me. "Smile," he commanded. As soon as I did so, they chorused again, "It's him." With that they let me go back to the bus.

It didn't take me long to discern the lesson in this little incident. Together with the lessons from the two men who were joyful in spite of their handicap, I deduced that the Lord intended for me to be joyful and smile. I had been misrepresenting the Christian life for many years.

But I still didn't know *how* to be happy. To smile when I wasn't happy seemed hypocritical to me. I had never studied about joy in the Bible. I had only studied about sorrow. I had plenty of ammunition to defend a gloomy appearance. Jesus was "a man of sorrows, and acquainted with grief" (Isa. 53:3).

I took comfort in Psalm 34:18: "The Lord is nigh unto them that are of a broken heart." And I felt that "sorrow is better than laughter: for by the sadness of the countenance the heart is made better" (Eccl. 7:3). There are more of these types of verses, but I hadn't understood them correctly. Joy and sorrow are like two sides of the same coin, but the joy side should be up the majority of the time.

Proverbs 14:13 says, "Even in laughter the heart is sorrowful; and the end of that mirth is heaviness." Yet we need to put our best foot forward if we're ever going to make Christ attractive to others. Nehemiah 8:10 says, "Neither be ye sorry; for the joy of the Lord is your strength."

This was all fine, but I still couldn't force myself to be joyful. How could I have this joy? When I was in a relationship with a potential wife, I was happy. When the relationship failed, I was unhappy. This wasn't right because Jesus said in John 16:22 that "your joy no man taketh from you."

Then I found the answer in Psalm 16:11: "In thy presence is fulness of joy."

The Spirit of Prophecy says that the Lord's presence with us is directly proportional to our awareness of it. It's not easy to continually keep the mind on one thing. I went back to my Spirit of Prophecy statements about Enoch and discovered his secret of walking with God. Enoch prayed continually. He constantly dwelt upon the goodness, kindness, and perfection of the character of God. He kept his attention on things not seen. These principles are obvious enough, but how many of us are doing them? I sure wasn't. My mind wanted to dwell upon earthly things and supposed difficulties. I was so desperate because of loneliness and lack of joy that I enlisted the grace of God in order to give this a try. Every time my mind started to wander, as soon as I recognized this happening, I brought my thoughts back to the reality that the presence of the Holy Spirit was in and around me. You know, it brought a genuine smile to my face. When no one was looking, I was smiling. When everyone was looking, I was smiling.

I spoke about this experience at a church in Eastern Europe. A nice woman told me that she liked my talk, and she seemed to be somewhat interested in me as well. I tried to start a relationship with her, but after a couple of interactions with her, she rejected me. I fought to hold that joy of the Lord by keeping my mind stayed upon Him. It was a struggle not to fall into the pit of despair.

Soon after that some friends introduced me to another woman who had never been married but wanted to be. We got together a couple of times. She was friendly and hospitable. I hoped this relationship would blossom into something permanent.

One night before I was to see her, I had a very short dream just as I was dozing off to sleep. I dreamed that a large butterfly flew right into my face. When I say large, I mean about eight or ten inches across. It was all white. The dream startled me so much that I immediately woke up. I remembered the dream very clearly. I was impressed that the Lord was telling me that He had brought me or soon would bring me face to face with my "butterfly," or future wife.

Now I needed to know if it was or was not the woman I was currently seeing. She didn't seem very serious about a steady relationship. Sunday morning I prayed for three hours, seeking God's will. I got the idea to make a large white paper butterfly. I made some design markings on it. Then on one wing I wrote "yes," and on the other wing I wrote "no." I put it in a self-addressed envelope.

That Sunday as this woman and I were having lunch together, I told her how God had assured me that He would find me a mate, just as He does for the butterflies. I told her about my dream. I gave her the envelope with the butterfly in it. I told her that if she decided that she wanted to build a relationship with me with the intention of marriage to circle yes on the wing; if not, she should circle no and send the butterfly to me. I told her to take her time to decide but not to wait too long. She agreed to do this. She lived in the capital city, and I lived in another city a couple of hours away. I went back home to await her reply.

****

It was on my first visit to Eastern Europe that I met Titi and Lisa. They were working as staff at an orphanage near where I was living.

In fact, the first time I saw Titi he was delivering the sermon at church. I was impressed with his solemn, earnest demeanor. I was introduced to Titi, and he invited me to come to the orphanage and talk to the children. While I was there, I was impressed to give some money to Titi and Lisa.

A little while after I gave Titi the money, he came to me privately. He was a little emotional as he told me that he and Lisa had never had a place to live in of their own. They worked at the orphanage before they got married and had been there ever since they were married. He said they had been saving up to get a place of their own, but they gave away some of their savings to help some worthy cause for the Lord. Then he told me, "The money you gave me is exactly ten times the amount we gave to the Lord."

After I returned to America, I learned that Titi and Lisa had finally moved out of the orphanage, and Titi was working at the printing house for Eugen. The printing house burned down soon after that, and Titi and Lisa were forced to move into

The Seven Thunders

his mother's apartment in another city. This is when I first found out that Titi had a sister. Titi and Lisa, the sister and her child, and the mother and another man were all living in a two-bedroom apartment. It wasn't good for the privacy Titi and Lisa needed. They were the only practicing Christians in the household, which made things difficult, and to top it off, Lisa was soon to give birth.

I continued to send money to help Titi and Lisa because he was unemployed. Jobs were very hard to find in that country, especially in the winter.

I was not aware that some of the money was being shared with Titi's sister and her daughter for food and things. I knew very little about Titi's sister, not even her name.

On my second visit to that country, I got a glimpse of Titi's sister when Eugen, the woman I thought I was going to marry, and I stopped at the apartment to see Titi.

On my third visit to that country, I saw Titi's sister on a few occasions when she came to visit Titi and Lisa who were now living in the same city where I was. Once I saw her at the mother's apartment when Titi and I stopped in for a few minutes. In fact, I was playing catch with Lana's daughter when she happened to walk into the living room. Lana never even looked at me, and no one introduced us.

I had been praying for Lana after the first time I learned that Titi had a sister. I normally do this for my friends' families. I knew only that she had had a hard life and was separated from her husband who had been perpetually unfaithful to her.

As Titi and I were working together at the printing house, I heard a little news about his sister now and then. When she had a dream about the world ending soon, Titi came to work and told us about it.

I remember the time that Lana came to visit Titi and Lisa after having that dream. I saw her in church with them. That was the time I took a long, hard look at Lana. I wasn't particularly attracted to her looks or deportment, although I thought that she was very pleasant looking. As I was looking at Lana, the thought came into my mind, "You're looking at your future wife." It didn't really fit in with the train of my thoughts at that moment. It was rather a disconnected thought, seemingly out of nowhere. I looked harder at her and told myself, "No, she doesn't look like the type for me." She didn't look happy, and she wasn't an Adventist, so I dismissed the thought that she would ever be my wife.

I had heard of people having the same thought about someone that, in fact, did become their spouse, but I thought that it wasn't going to turn out that way for me. It was in August of 1999 when I saw Lana in the church and had that thought about her.

One day, about the end of the next month, I was at work at the printing house. Titi was running the big press, and I was folding pages. Titi spoke up, "Curt, my sister accepted Jesus Christ as her personal Savior."

"Oh, how did that come about?" I asked.

"She gave her heart to God during the NET '99 meetings by evangelist Mark Finley," he said.

I thanked God for working a miracle in his sister's life, but I didn't think much more about it at the time. The thought did cross my mind that perhaps I could meet her sometime, but because of the way the other women had rejected me, I didn't think there was much possibility in Titi's sister having an interest in me. She wasn't really what I was looking for anyway.

A short time later Titi announced that he and Lisa were returning to work for the orphanage, this time in a distant town from where we were currently living.

I remarked to Titi that with him moving away I would probably never get a chance to be introduced to his sister. I was waiting for a response from Titi to that remark, but he was strangely silent.

I had become good friends with a young Adventist man named Sorin Sonea and his girlfriend, Amalia Mihaila. They, like Eugen and his wife, Julia, and Titi and Lisa, had genuine compassion for me. They understood my loneliness. Sorin and Amy were on the lookout for a woman for me.

When we went places together, Amy would put her arm in mine and in Sorin's and we would walk along that way. That act made me feel really good. Sometimes when we parted, Amy would kiss my cheeks as is the custom among friends in Eastern Europe, but I could sense a real gesture of good will from her.

I was having more joy in the Lord than ever before, but the longing for a wife to share my life with, as a good friend and mate, left a longing in my heart.

It was during the time that I was waiting for the woman from the capital city to send me her decision on the wings of the paper butterfly I had given her that Sorin came to my apartment one evening. He was very exited about something. He said that there were some evangelistic meetings coming up soon in a nearby town. They were going to be on archaeology and the Bible, as presented by a British evangelist. Sorin had already met this man, who was there preparing for the meetings. There was to be another preparatory meeting on Wednesday, and Sorin wanted me to go with him to meet the English-speaking evangelist.

Wednesday came along and Sorin, Amy, and I hitchhiked and then rode a tram to get to the church in the nearby town.

The nearby town was actually a fairly large city of approximately one hundred thousand people—there are four Seventh-day Adventist churches there. We had a little difficulty finding the church where the meeting was to take place, but we arrived just before it was to start.

I noticed a small group of people seated at the front left corner of the sanctuary. They were just ending some kind of a meeting and began to move to other seats for the evangelist's meeting.

I watched one young woman coming up the aisle. She looked familiar. I thought she looked like Titi's sister, but there was something different about her appearance, and I wasn't sure. I had seen Eugen's father at the rear of the sanctuary, so with Sorin to interpret, we went back to ask him if that was indeed Titi's sister. She had taken a seat on the far left toward the rear of the sanctuary. Victor, Eugen's father, peered over at her, then he took out his glasses to get a better look. He indicated that he believed that it was Titi's sister. I marched right over and stood just behind and to the right of where she was seated. I greeted her and asked her if she knew who I was. I spoke in English, not knowing if she understood any. I pointed to myself and said, "I'm Titi's friend." It was then that I first learned that her name was Lana. She nodded in recognition and reached for her purse in the seat next to her as though she was making a place for me to sit. I promptly took the cue and sat next to her.

Since the presentation was given in English and the local language, we both understood the message. Throughout the presentation, Lana and I looked at each other with alternating looks of interest, wonderment, or mirth. We met again and again, same time, same place, as the meetings continued night after night.

The small meeting up in front of the sanctuary that first Wednesday evening had been for baptismal preparation. Lana was preparing to make a public commitment to turn her back on sin and this world and live for Christ.

At first I wasn't sure if it was going to be Lana or the woman from the capital city. But the butterfly arrived a few days after Lana and I met, and the "NO" on the wing was underlined.

I didn't waste much time in letting Lana know that I was searching for a wife and that I would be interested in marrying her if we discovered we were happy together. She said that she was open and favorable to that idea.

As Lana and I reviewed the developments that led up to our relationship, we were impressed that no one had ever introduced us although we had been in situations where that would have been appropriate and rather expected. We concluded that this way God received the credit for bringing us together. We believe that God prepared us for each other in His way, and in His time.

With only about three or four months left to my stay in Eastern Europe, I didn't think there would be enough time to build a loving relationship with a woman and get married. Because of financial concerns it was imperative that I return to America in early spring.

I had doubted God's love for me. I had doubted the ability of God to do the seemingly impossible. I was determined not to return to America alone.

I was like Thomas, the doubting disciple. But now like Thomas I had seen God's hand and I believed in His promises. Like Thomas my testimony is, "My Lord and my God!" (John 20:28).

Chapter 13

MANY THANKS, LORD

Lana and I were married for nearly eleven years. Most of those years were the best of my life. We did many things together. We traveled and hiked. We worked and bought a house together. Sadly, something changed in Lana. She said that she could no longer live with me and abruptly left.

Once again I found myself disappointed, sad, and lonely. Once again I was not exhibiting "the joy of the Lord." How could I attract others to the Savior with the lines of sadness and loneliness written across my brow?

In fact, one of the reasons Lana gave for leaving was that I didn't smile enough. I admit that the coldness and selfishness of others has a big impact on me. When Lana would do something that I considered selfish, I found it hard to smile.

Again I went back to God for the solution to my problem. I'm relating these events in my life in order to show how we can have victory in our lives amidst discouraging circumstances. God allows trials for one specific reason, to purify our character and prepare us to meet Him. God hates divorce. I never dreamed I would find myself in this situation.

When all this happened, people told me I married the wrong person. They told me I married for the wrong reasons. Church members told me I should not have gone looking for a mate. Some told me that our relationship progressed too fast, that I should have waited a long time to get to know Lana better. One said that because I tried to find a wife the devil answered my prayers.

If any or all of these are true, then my relationship with God is one big mass of confusion. If those criticisms are true, then I don't know God at all. Why do I say this? Look at this statement: "We should now acquaint ourselves with God by proving His promises" (*The Great Controversy*, p. 622). As far as I am concerned, I was learning to know God by observing the way He works in fulfilling His Word through the Bible promises. As we cooperate with God in selecting His opening providences, we not only receive the gift that is in the promise but we learn valuable lessons on God's character and manner of working with people. Once we have learned these principles of God's dealing with us, we have an example to emulate in our dealings with others.

We only know "about" Jesus until we practice His lessons. Then it is that we "actually" know Him because we become an extension of His love. Then we are abiding in Him.

Jesus abode in the Father through serving others. Jesus did it by emulating the manner of the Father's working that He had Himself learned by proving God's promises. He first learned to use the promises to maintain a vital connection with God and then utilized the same method in working to uplift humanity. If it was not the Lord that I was becoming acquainted with by claiming the various promises for a wife, then I have nothing to offer anyone, and you would be well advised to toss this book in the trash.

Many people claim that since my marriage ended in divorce it could not have been the Lord that led me into the marriage. I pondered that for some time. I was led to review the Lord's dealings as outlined in His Word. I remembered that it was God who formed Adam's wife for him. But Eve helped lead Adam into sin. Should we conclude that Adam should never have married Eve? Job's wife said to Job, "Curse God and die." Should we conclude that Job was not perfect as God said he was, because he obviously chose a wife other than the one God would have chosen for him?

For several months after Lana left me, I poured over the Bible and Spirit of Prophecy statements in an effort to ascertain an understanding of how God answers prayer. I wanted to know the science of how "prayer moves the arm of Omnipotence" (*Testimonies for the Church,* vol. 5, p. 453). I found out that circumstances are to be our helpers, not hindrances. I had been feeling like a victim of my circumstances. My circumstances were dictating my moods.

I took a promise found in Romans 8:28—"And we know that all things work together for good to them that love God, to them who are the called according to his purpose"—and began to build upon that promise. My circumstances were going to become my helpers rather than my hindrances. I decided to put into practice the science of prayer. Look at this statement: "Prayer and faith are closely allied, and they need to be studied together. In the prayer of faith there is a divine science; it is a science that everyone who would make his life-work a success must understand. Christ says, 'What things soever ye desire, when ye pray, believe that ye receive them, and ye shall have them.' Mark 11:24. He makes it plain that our asking must be according to God's will; we must ask for the things that He has promised, and whatever we receive must be used in doing His will. The conditions met, the promise is unequivocal" (*Maranatha,* p. 87).

I was determined that something good must come out of my circumstances. I had already learned that I must rest my confidence in God's love for me even if He didn't grant my request right away.

One more thing was needful, though, in my experience. I still found myself being a poor specimen of a joyful Christian by wearing a long face most of the time. I came upon this statement: "Educate yourself to carry a pleasant countenance, and bring all the sweetness and melody possible into your voice" (*The Adventist Home*, p. 432). Here was an almost absurd thought to me. Does God mean I must force myself to wear a smile when it is not welling-up naturally from within? Wouldn't that be phony? Well the Lord never makes a mistake, so I decided to give it a try. Something remarkable began to happen. Now, mind you, I enlisted divine aid to help me do this. Nevertheless, as I kept reminding myself to smile, it actually became easier. The smile (it kind of looks like a smirk because of my facial lines) began to stick around even when I wasn't forcing it. Furthermore, it didn't seem phony because it caused me to think more about His presence within which is the "fulness of joy" (Ps. 16:11). It also reminded me to thank Him for His promises. There is an added dimension and blessing as well. People started acting friendlier toward me. Thanks be to God!

Although I didn't enjoy living alone, I experienced joy in the ability to travel, which is something I love to do. I like to see and experience different cultures, and I like to meet new people and make new friends. A blessing came when I was selected to go to China twice in 2011 for the company I worked for.

I smiled and made many friends there. One of the persons I met was a man from Britain who worked for the hotel where I stayed both times. He was the manager and head chef for one of the restaurants in the hotel. I shared with him about the divorce I was in the middle of, and I told him that I would like to eventually remarry if circumstances permitted it. He told me that he had a Philippine wife who was loyal and submissive to a fault. He told me that he knew for a fact that the Indonesian and Malaysian women were the same way. It is their culture. The Western world has lost something beautiful. It is called God's "original design." It consists of the submissive wife and the benevolent husband combination, which is biblical. After listening to the chef, I was convinced of where I would take a wife if ever the Lord opened the way to do so.

The trips to China only served to whet my appetite to travel more and to share the Word of God with others—I discreetly spread some Christian tracts around while in China. I asked for a month off from work and was granted my request. I began asking the Lord to open up the way to go on a mission trip of some sort. I wanted to go someplace where the people would welcome the opportunity to lift them up spiritually. In the West it seems as if people receive the gospel contemptuously as if tasting bad medicine. They want the least dosage to get them by.

I applied to four different ministries to accept me on missionary efforts that they had scheduled for November 2011. My preference was to go to Northern India or the Philippines. I was turned down for those. I was offered a spot in Brazil near the Amazon River but that was for construction work. I wanted to do evangelism. Then *Quiet Hours Ministry* accepted me to go to the Island of Borneo. I wasn't really attracted to Borneo until I found out that it comprises a part of Malaysia.

My selfish heart immediately thought of the loyal, submissive women there. That was not my main motive for choosing that trip, but after all, they had accepted me, hadn't they? They were touting the trip as a potentially "life changing" event. Well, that is exactly what I was looking for. And that is exactly what I received, thanks to God! I feel compelled to tell about it. It is my primary motive for writing this chapter. The unfolding of the whole experience only added to my admiration of God's character. I hope it does the same for you. Now I claim promises constantly. I do so because I want to become better acquainted with my Lord and Savior Jesus Christ.

The following statement brought me great comfort. It fit my situation so perfectly—I am simple enough to believe that it was penned just for me.

"In order to receive the precious gifts of God, we must meet Him upon the platform of His own devising, complying with the conditions that He has laid down in His word. There is much turning aside from the word of God. Because iniquity abounds, the love of many waxes cold. When a trial of faith comes upon those that profess to be the children of God, they do not perseveringly present their petitions before the throne of mercy, depending upon the Holy Spirit, waiting and watching, and continuing to present their requests, searching the Scriptures at the same time to know what is the mind of God. Place your feet in the path of God's commandments, and be assured that your prayers will be answered. There is a great lack of earnestness, a great lack of vital interest in prayer. Yet we are exhorted to be 'instant in prayer,' 'to pray without ceasing.' We are to keep a spirit of intercession, and present all our wants to God. We are to tell Him about the smallest things of life,—our cares, our business, our desires and needs. You can never weary the Lord by your importuning. It is by beholding Jesus that you become changed into the divine similitude. We may behold Him by continuing in prayer, until we are not aware that we are praying; for our souls turn to the Sun of Righteousness as a flower turns to the light" (*The Signs of the Times,* May 28, 1896).

Here is another quote that I took to heart: "We must not only pray in Christ's name, but by the inspiration of the Holy Spirit. This explains what is meant when it is said that the Spirit 'maketh intercession for us, with groanings which cannot be uttered.' Romans 8:26. Such prayer God delights to answer. When with earnestness and intensity we breathe a prayer in the name of Christ, there is in that very intensity a pledge from God that He is about to answer our prayer 'exceeding abundantly above all that we ask or think.' Ephesians 3:20" (*Christ's Object Lessons*, p. 147).

We are talking about getting our prayers answered. That is what I want and wanted. Here was another situation that seemed odd to me, just like forcing a smile when I didn't really feel like it. How was I to add intensity and earnestness to my prayers? Should I work myself up into a frenzy? Should I shout it at the top of my lungs? Those two approaches didn't seem very reverent. Looking again at the first part of the statement, I noticed that our prayers must be inspired by the Holy Spirit. I asked God to give me intensity of desire. I asked the Lord to inspire me with His Holy Spirit and for intensity and earnestness in my prayers. Since all of God's biddings are enablings, anything I lack He is ready to supply. My prayer was that I might be able to share my testimony in Malaysia and that God would enhance my testimony about Him by supplying a life-changing blessing there. My earnestness and intensity was buoyed and inspired by the Holy Spirit through the encouragement of these Spirit of Prophecy statements:

"So with all the promises of God's Word. In them He is speaking to us individually, speaking as directly as if we could listen to His voice. It is in these promises that Christ communicates to us His grace and power. They are leaves from that tree which is 'for the healing of the nations.' Received, assimilated, they are to be the strength of the character, the inspiration and sustenance of the life" (*The Faith I Live By*, p. 9).

"The Bible is God's voice speaking to us just as surely as though we could hear Him with our ears. The word of the living God is not merely written, but spoken. Do we receive the Bible as the oracle of God? If we realized the importance of this Word, with what awe would we open it, and with what earnestness would we search its precepts. The reading and contemplating of the Scriptures would be regarded as an audience with the Most High" (*In Heavenly Places*, p. 134).

"We are to open the Word of God with reverence and with a sincere desire to know the will of God concerning us. The heavenly angels will direct our search. God speaks to us in His Word. We are in the audience chamber of the Most High, in the very presence of God. Christ enters the heart" (*My Life Today*, p. 283).

I reminded the Lord when I claimed each promise that He had just looked me in the eyes and spoken in my ears a promise. I reverently told the Lord that He is only as good as His Word; I told Him that He boasts that He cannot lie and never changes. With that I told the Lord that I fully expected to receive the gifts that are in the promises I had claimed. I appropriated the promises to my circumstances. I asked God to do it. I told Him I believed He could and would do it. I sealed the pact by thanking Him in advance for having already done it.

The trip started out a little less than optimally when I missed my second flight by a matter of a few minutes. The really sad part was that I was right next to the gate of my departure the whole time. I ended up having to redo my whole itinerary. It not only cost me an extra hundred dollars but also would make me late for the start of the evangelistic meetings I was to be taking part in. I ended up having to sit at the Portland airport for an additional twelve hours. That definitely threatened to wipe the smile off my face. My only recourse was to take my complaint to God, which I did.

As it turned out, by a twist of circumstances, (by the way, I used the opportunity to make my circumstance my helper and not my hindrance by inviting God to once again bring something good out of a seemingly bad situation) I arrived on time for the first meeting in Sabah, Borneo. The airline even gave me a voucher for a hotel room and free lunch, the value of which were probably about the amount I had to pay extra. I was able to freshen up before arriving at my final destination. Any long distance traveler will appreciate the value of that. And on the last leg of my trip, I was able to witness to a Malaysian woman. This would not have occurred had I made my original flight.

Once I arrived in Malaysia, I met the other people helping with the meetings. We had six teams for six churches where we would be preaching and teaching. I was assigned as a helper to Werner Grob, a wonderful Christian man. Werner and I were assigned to a church that was probably the most remote of them all. Many of the congregants were illiterate.

I immediately fell in love with the people, especially the children. I had taken little toys to give them, so they naturally began to sit with me at the meetings. Some of them were quite characters. They would play little tricks on me and make strange faces at me. It was very amusing.

We were assigned a driver to bring us back and forth to the church from our lodging, which incidentally was quite crude but adequate and comfortable. We stayed in a "longhouse" assembled of posts, bamboo slats, and a thatched roof. A simple mattress on the floor with a mosquito net suspended over it comprised the furnishings. Toilets and showers were a short walk away.

Our driver's name was Enjau. He only had one good eye and drove very slowly and cautiously. Werner always made sure that we began our trips with a word of prayer. At first Enjau wasn't accustomed to waiting for prayer before pulling away.

Unfailingly, though, Werner's big hands would reach for Enjau's shoulder, and he would offer a simple but pointed prayer in his charming German brogue. It went invariably like this: "Many thanks, dear Lord, for our chauffer. You know that he has one dead eye. We pray that you would restore it. We pray that you would watch over us on the way."

Immediately following the first meeting at the church, many members, both male and female, asked me if I was married. Apparently this is the customary question in their country. "My wife left me about a year ago," was my reply. The available women stayed by while the men folk wandered away. One woman asked me if I was on Facebook. "No, but I'll trade you e-mail addresses," I said. We did so. Her name was Julima. I had already noticed this woman. She was in charge of playing the recorded hymn music for the singing. Of course, I didn't know she was unmarried until she talked to me after the meeting.

The next day they sent me to a different church whose main speaker didn't have a helper. I was told that would be my assignment from then on. I didn't enjoy it there as much as at Nangka, the more remote church. I liked the people at the first church. I also wanted to get to know Julima better. So I asked one of the coordinators if I could go back to the Nangka church, and she said yes.

Someone might be thinking I was trying to put my own interest before the Lord's. I prefer to think of it as combining our interests. I have thought the situation over carefully. I have weighed the choices I made against the way the situation unfolded. I have prayed extensively about it. I am convinced that the way things turned out is exactly the way it was supposed to be. It's a long story if I were to give all of the details.

As it turned out, on succeeding nights I was able to share some of the things I have related in this book. The Lord made it clear to me that I had not made a mistake in discerning His leading. I still had a valid testimony to share.

Something also happened at the meetings that still baffles me. They asked me if I would do special music, which could mean only one thing—singing a solo. Unfortunately, I don't have much of a singing voice. The part that baffles me is that I agreed to do it. I had never done that before, but I actually enjoyed it. To my utter surprise, so did they. In fact, I (I should be saying "we" every time I say "I," meaning the Lord and I) sang on four different occasions! This was a groundbreaking experience for me. Had I continued on at the other church I may not have realized this blessing.

In the meantime, I tried to talk with Julima a little bit each night. I inquired about her family. I found out that she lived with her father. Julima's father had not been coming to the meetings, so I informed Julima that I wanted to visit her father. I wanted to give him a personal invitation to attend the meetings. Also in the meantime, I gathered all the information I could about Julima from other church members. This came about partly because Julima herself hardly said a word to me. I was starting to think that Julima had no genuine interest in me after all. Ordinarily this is all it would have taken for me to feel rejected and immediately desist from pursuing her. Here, then, was another "first" for me. For some strange reason, I felt compelled to continue pursuing her.

Sabbath arrived. This was the day that I told Julima I wanted to visit her father. As people were leaving after church and potluck, I spied Julima also walking away. I quickly rushed over and told her I wanted to go meet her father. Once again she seemed to brush me off.

I immediately came up with a plan B. I was staying around the church area until the evening meeting instead of going back to the lodge to rest for the afternoon, so I decided to go for a long walk through the countryside to enjoy nature and God's creative power. And I would have to walk right past Julima's house on the way. My hope was that she would see me and have a change of heart. I walked right past and continued walking. My plan was to walk for one hour, then turn around and walk back. After almost half an hour, a pickup came driving up the road behind me. I didn't pay any attention to it until it pulled up beside me. I looked in and there was Julima and Julia, another woman from church. There had been several ways I could have taken. I'm not sure how they found me. Actually, they never admitted to looking for me to begin with. Anyway, at that moment I knew the tide had turned, the ice was broken.

"Where are you going?" they asked.

"I'm just walking. Where are you going?" I responded.

"We're just driving," they said.

"May I ride with you?" I asked.

"Sure," they said.

I suppose I could just say right here that "the rest is history." But since this is an historical account and also a testimony of God's love and care, I'd rather provide a detailed historical record.

We ended up going back to Julia's house—her husband is an elder at the church. After a bit we went for a walk, and some of Julia's family joined us. On the way back, as Julima had moved ahead, I tarried behind to talk to Julia. She asked me if I was interested in marrying Julima. I assured her that I was. I asked her why Julima had never been married.

"No one has asked her," she replied.

"She's a nice looking woman," I added with a puzzled look as I thought about her statement. Then I added, "I don't think she's interested in me."

"Whoever wants to marry her, him will she love," Julia stated.

"Do you think she would marry me," I asked as I looked up the road where I could see Julima. She was kind of frolicking as she marched along.

"Yes, I think she would," Julia said reassuringly.

I had observed Julima closely. She had little behaviors I liked and were similar to my own. She could snatch up a little bantam hen before it knew what happened to it. She liked to grab green fruit off the tree and chew on it. She is modest, hard working, generous, cheerful, dependable, loyal, conservative, non-complaining. She also loves the outdoors, flowers, animals, children, and doing crafts. She is intelligent, thoughtful, and has a good sense of humor. There is one more thing that stands out as a beautiful character trait in Julima in my eyes. She does not hesitate to say she is sorry when she thinks she has offended someone.

Julima found out that I had more than just a casual interest in her, and we began texting each other. She asked me why I would want an Asian woman over an American one. That was easy for me to answer. I told her she was different than the American women in many ways, ways that meant all the difference to me. I sent a picture of Julima and I to my sister Phyllis. Phyllis observed what was already speaking to my own heart. She said, "Julima looks like the wife you always should have had."

After the meetings were over, I was scheduled to fly to West Malaysia to do some sightseeing. I still had spoken very little to Julima in person. We were texting regularly, but I didn't really know her. We hadn't spent any time together just her and I. From West Malaysia I went north into Thailand for a few days. Afterward, I came back to Malaysia from where I was to depart for home in a couple of days. I really missed Julima. I wanted to see her again before going home. How, after all, could I make any decisions or plans based on such a brief and superficial acquaintance?

So I decided to change my plans and fly back to Borneo Island. I extended my stay so that Julie, as Julima prefers to go by, and I had about three days to spend with each other. During that time, which was wonderful, I became more convinced than ever that Julie was the one for me. I saw God's hand at work in our relationship. I let Julie know that I wanted her for my wife. I asked her if she thought her father would agree to let me marry her. She said she didn't know.

We were down to mere hours left to spend with each other. We went down to the river together. The same river where I had watched many individuals be baptized as a result of our meetings. The river that Julie swam in. The river that, during one of our texting sessions, an interruption occurred, prompting this message, "Must rescue buffalo, river flooding…" The river that I had longed to swim in with Julie.

What a life, I thought, *out in nature, swimming whenever one feels like it, growing your own food and living off the land. Julie, you don't know how blessed you are, far removed from the stressful, hustle and bustle of the city, and might I add, the American life.*

The Lord had heard the innocent desire of my heart and out of His great heart of compassion had granted me the thing I longed for. It was there at the river, in storybook fashion, that I received my answer from Julie. I was treading water while admiring Julie sitting on a nearby rock. She was fixing her long, jet-black hair while watching me having fun in the water. "My father said it is alright for you to marry me," she suddenly said.

"That's great that he said yes," I replied. "But what about you?" I searched her face for an indication of some sort. She held my gaze with her deep, brown eyes. Finally, after what seemed like an eternity, which indicated the carefulness of her decision, she said, "Yes."

I tell you there is nothing like being on cloud 9 when you've been down in the lowlands for any length of time. I jumped up and swept Julie off the rock and into the water, clothes and all. I had to show my jubilation somehow. Meanwhile I thanked the Lord for His great mercies. I didn't deserve such a gift from the Lord, but I was reminded of this message that the Lord wrote to all who will receive it: "He that spared not his own Son, but delivered him up for us all, how shall he not with him also freely give us all things?" (Rom. 8:32).

Chapter 14

GOD'S SURE PROMISES

I shouldn't have to, but I feel compelled to preface this chapter with an effort to stave off what may come as well-intentioned criticism of its content. I believe, and will always believe, that I am a sinner in need of a Savior. I believe in absolute and total surrender and dependency upon God our Father and the Lord Jesus Christ through the indwelling of the Holy Spirit. I don't claim any special privilege or gifts from God. I don't want to be well known nor do I want to be quoted or eluded to as any kind of an authority on anything.

My Lord Jesus Christ is all in all. This is written to exalt Him and to magnify His Word and His holy law of the Ten Commandments. Maybe what I'm going to share is already common knowledge, but I don't think so. When God shared this understanding with me, it came with such clarity, force, and suddenness that I had to almost catch my breath.

I share it here and now because I have met and talked to so many people who attend church or who wish they could be a Christian but don't know how to fall in love with Jesus or trust His Word.

There was the time, for example, when I walked into a man's jail cell and he burst into tears. He told me he desperately wanted to be a Christian. He said his mother was a praying woman. He told me he wanted to love God with all of his heart, but he said, "I just don't feel anything in my heart for God."

I told him that he couldn't feel anything in his heart for God because he was trying to do it with his old sinful, stony heart. I showed him in Ezekiel 36:26 where it says that God will give us a new heart and with that heart we can love God. He asked God for the new heart, and the power of God and His Word changed that young man's experience.

It didn't come without great effort and pleading with God to learn what I have learned. Maybe others have learned this as easy as you please, but I have had savage battles with doubts and mistrust of God's love. I rather think, though, that my experience is typical. The problem is that most people don't push the battle through to victory. Many lay dying on the battlefield now, and many have already died.

Perhaps this testimony of my experience will come to the attention of a few for whom there is still hope. Perhaps they will be encouraged to obtain the victory over doubt, fear, and distrust.

Jesus Himself, though He never succumbed to these things, still fought against them, the same way that we must—"with strong crying and tears" unto God (Heb. 5:7). Jacob wrestled all night and was injured in battle before he gained the victory.

The doubts and fears I'm primarily talking about are not that my salvation is not sure, not that I don't have a mansion in heaven prepared for me. I haven't had a great problem with doubting that God could keep me from any particular sin. In spite of the fact that Jesus died for my sins two thousand years ago and the enormity of the love expressed there, I struggled with doubting His present day love for me. I've had so much trouble and disappointment since becoming a Christian that I didn't think God cared about the needs of my heart. I doubted the scriptures that promised present day temporal blessings and fulfillment. God slowly brought me out of that doubt, and now I offer this testimony to encourage others.

When the angel (Christ) laid a hand on Jacob on that night of wrestling, Jacob thought it was an enemy who had accosted him. He struggled with all his strength to break free from his assailant. Finally, in desperation, as his utter guilt and hopelessness were impressed upon him, Jacob made an entire surrender to God. It was then that he realized that the One who he thought was his enemy was really his Savior. Jacob then fought with all of his strength to hold on to the angel who was now trying to break free from Jacob.

There is a great spiritual lesson here for us. Many children of God are going through this process without realizing it. It doesn't usually happen in one night as with Jacob, but it is happening nonetheless. The problem is that most of us don't recognize this process for what it is. Many are losing their way when, if they had a clear knowledge of what was truly transpiring, they would press on to victory.

The Desire of Ages was the second book I read by Ellen White. I found it in a secondhand store not long after I found *The Great Controversy* in the public library. For many years now, I have been reading *The Desire of Ages* on an unending basis. As soon as I finish it, I start it again. It has helped me to understand the Scriptures in a very profound way. On page 390 it says, concerning Bible study, "We should take one verse, and concentrate the mind on the task of ascertaining the thought which God has put in that verse for us. We should dwell upon the thought until it becomes our own, and we know 'what saith the Lord.' In His promises and warnings, Jesus means me. The experiences related in God's word are to be my experiences. Prayer and promise, precept and warning, are mine."

I began to look at the experiences of different people in the Bible. I endeavored to discover the principles that were an issue in these experiences. Then I began to see the same principles being tested in my own life. A pattern began to develop. I could see some of the experiences of David, Samson, Jacob, Joseph, and others in my own experience. The circumstances are, of course, different, but they are basically the same experiences because of the principles involved.

Many Christians, Seventh-day Adventists as well, are not pursuing this kind of a relationship to the Bible. They read the stories in the Bible, but that is as far as it goes. The only difference we must insist upon in making the experiences recorded in the Bible our own is to have victory where the Bible character failed. "Now all these things happened unto them for examples: and they are written for our admonition, upon whom the ends of the world are come" (1 Cor. 10:11).

God used a Buddhist in Malaysia to confirm these thoughts. The man was a desk clerk at a youth hostel at which I stayed for one night. He was an interesting man who seemed to take a personal interest in all of his tenants. He engaged me in conversation every time I went into the lobby area. He asked me all about my life. After learning that I was a Christian, he made an insightful observation. He said, "Mr. Curtis, you are a Christian." I nodded. "You read the Holy Bible, is that correct? Again, I nodded. "Is it so that there are many experiences recorded in the Bible?" he asked.

"Yes there are," I answered.

"Mr. Curtis, those experiences are to be your experiences," he said. He couldn't have been more correct. This insightful man was confirming what the Lord had been impressing upon me for some time. He reminded me that I needed to look into God's Word to find out what or whose experience was being played out in my life at that very time period.

One exciting thing I have learned is that because of the office of Jesus as High Priest in the heavenly sanctuary I can enter intelligently and deliberately into the process of my sanctification. God wants our cooperation, not only through our willingness but through our understanding also. God doesn't always reveal everything to us ahead of time because it wouldn't be a genuine test that way, but we can begin to see in all of our circumstances a pattern. It brings great comfort to the soul to know that God is preparing us for our eternal home. It is a most holy place that Jesus has gone to prepare for us. We must gain a most holy experience and character in order to appreciate heaven. That is why we must enter willingly into the most holy place of the heavenly sanctuary where Jesus officiates and cooperate with Him in the work of sanctification—character-building.

I have been very careful not to ask for the experience of someone in the Bible if it involved a great trial. I prayed for trials once and that cured me of wanting to do that again. I found that by praying for certain promises, I get the preparatory trial for receiving that gift anyway.

On page 123 of *The Desire of Ages* it says, "Every promise in God's word is ours." That statement, along with the one quoted above from page 390, tells me that no matter whom the promise was originally given to I can claim it as my own.

It's not hard to claim promises. Most Christians have claimed God's promises. Sadly, many lose faith when they don't receive the gift in the promise. The way to receive the gift is hardly ever mentioned by those who encourage us to claim God's promises. After claiming promises for a few years and never receiving the gift, many in our churches fall back into an indifferent attitude toward them, although they probably wouldn't admit that they don't trust God to keep all of His promises. Some claim the promise of forgiveness but don't claim the promises for victory over sin.

This is more than just a casual, superficial problem. It is eating the heart out of our churches. Ellen White wrote, "As witnesses for Christ, we are to tell what we know, what we ourselves have seen and heard and felt. If we have been following Jesus step by step, we shall have something right to the point to tell concerning the way in which He has led us. We can tell how we have tested His promise, and found the promise true. We can bear witness to what we have known of the grace of Christ. This is the witness for which our Lord calls, and for want of which the world is perishing" (*The Desire of Ages*, p. 340).

I'd like to add that not only is the world perishing because we haven't learned to test God's promises and receive the gift, but many of the young people in our churches are dead spiritually because we adults don't have a testimony of victory after victory to share with them.

Once again, I repeat what it says in *The Great Controversy*, "We should now acquaint ourselves with God by proving His promises" (p. 622). If we are not claiming promises and receiving definite answers, not only do we not have a testimony that the world needs, but we don't even have an acquaintance with God, whom we claim to know.

While in Eastern Europe I met a 17-year-old girl who went to church with her mother. She was a charming girl who knew our doctrines exquisitely. I asked her if she was baptized, and she said, "No." I asked why not, and she said that she still has some questions about God. Later she told me she doesn't care if she goes to heaven or hell.

I had to ask myself what in my experience and testimony had failed to make Jesus attractive enough to this girl so that she would sacrifice all to have Him.

I went back to see her, and I shared about how I had tested God's promises and found them to be true. I recounted to her specific promises I had claimed and the exact, specific answers I had received. I told her what I knew of the grace of Christ.

She fixed a solemn gaze upon me, looking me square in the eyes, and said, "Tell me more." I told her of promises I was at that time claiming and which I expected soon to be answered. She told me to come back and let her know when they were answered. I did, and I told of God's great plan for His children and of His great desire for our present happiness and fulfillment. I watched as huge, lovely tears welled-up in her eyes and slid down her cheeks.

She is still wrestling with the One who has placed a hand upon her. More recently she asked me why God instructed the Israelites to slaughter men, women, and children when they conquered the Promised Land. You see, she thinks that the angel that has assailed her is her enemy—just as Jacob did. I can't blame her for wanting to be absolutely sure that God is pure love. If God was only 99 percent love, I fear that I, myself, would find an excuse not to serve Him.

My responsibility to this girl and everyone else in this world was pronounced thousands of years ago in the Abrahamic Covenant: "And in thee shall all families of the earth be blessed" (Gen. 12:3). I must do all in my God-given strength to reveal to others what I have discovered—that God is 100 percent pure love and is deeply concerned about our present happiness. It is true that the Lord allows wounds to come our way, yet He is right there to heal us of the wound that is working for our benefit. The Lord touched Jacob's thigh and wounded him, but He also healed him enough so that he could still walk. Hosea 6:1-3 is worth quoting here: "Come, and let us return unto the LORD: for he hath torn, and he will heal us; he hath smitten, and he will bind us up. After two days will he revive us: in the third day he will raise us up, and we shall live in his sight. Then shall we know, if we follow on to know the LORD: his going forth is prepared as the morning; and he shall come unto us as the rain, as the latter and former rain unto the earth." This is only one scripture example of many.

In reviewing my own life in the light of the Scriptures, I found that promises were being fulfilled for me before I knew God. I believe this is because there were Christians praying for me. I believe this also because a period of probationary grace is given to every soul with evidences of God's love strategically manifested, occasionally in extraordinary ways, to wake us up to His claims upon our lives.

My mother prayed for my father's conversion to Christ for many years. My father had no interest in God, yet God gave evidence that He was hunting for my father's soul. My mother told me that one day my father came home from work with a story to relate. It seems that he had answered a service call to repair a furnace in a warehouse and was working alone. He had the sensation that someone was watching him. He couldn't see anyone else around, but he happened to look up, and there was a large picture of Jesus, and it was as though He were looking down at my father. Other evidences came my father's way over the years until he finally succumbed to the onslaught of God's love.

It is evident to me that God's promises, in addition to being helps in all varieties of difficulties, can be utilized to navigate our lives in the direction we would like them to go, as long as we are fulfilling the commission that Jesus gave us—"Go ye therefore, and teach all nations, baptizing them in the name of the Father, and of the Son, and of the Holy Ghost: Teaching them to observe all things whatsoever I have commanded you: and, lo, I am with you always, even unto the end of the world. Amen" (Matt. 28:19, 20).

We must always be subject to God's overriding plan for our lives, but within that plan God gives us great latitude, through freedom of choice, according to our heart's desire. Sadly, many are kind of just drifting along listlessly, not making use of the treasury of promises that are within their reach. They are waiting for God to do something instead of putting to use the resources the Lord has provided for us to utilize in His service.

The Spirit of Prophecy tells us that we are to converse with God through the Scriptures. I know that God's Word is Him speaking to us. It was a new thought to me to understand that I could talk in return to God through His Word. The Holy Bible is a two-way medium.

The difference between reading the Bible and conversing with God through the Bible is one of attitude and perspective. As I have learned to converse with God through the Scriptures, they have taken on a new meaning and importance to me. I feel a new sense of power in them. This passage expresses better what I want to relay to you: "But to this man will I look, even to him that is poor and of a contrite spirit, and trembleth at my word" (Isa. 66:2).

The Holy Bible is a moderately sized volume as far as books go, yet I'm simple enough to believe that every child of God can find personal, intimate details of his or her life recorded there. For those of us alive and wanting to work for God, the promises are there prominently displayed and awaiting our choosing.

Jesus was 12 years old when He discovered that "in the volume of the book it is written of me" (Ps. 40:7). From that point on, the mystery of His mission began to open up to Him. *The Desire of Ages* talks about His experience on page 78 when He saw the sanctuary service acted and realized that the ceremony related to Him.

It took me forty-four years to come to a mature realization that, personally, my life is in the Scriptures too. It is not my place to tell anyone where their life is recorded in the Scriptures. It is a personal revelation from God that comes as a blessing, through a loving, intimate relationship with Him. It simply reveals how intimately and personally involved God is with our daily lives.

It is not a testing point of one's faith to be able to point at some Scripture and say, "That was written solely for me," or "There is my life record."

Let me go back and explain how I have learned to see my life in the Scriptures.

It all started after I realized that God had spoken to me through the phenomenon of thunder. I had concluded that it was God speaking long before I became a Christian. Then the Lord confirmed my belief when He led me to Psalm 81:7, which says, "Thou calledst in trouble, and I delivered thee; I answered thee in the secret place of thunder." "Secret place" from the original Hebrew means "protection, hidden place." "Thunder" represents God's Word. God's Word is our protection or hiding place from sin. "Thy word have I hid in mine heart, that I might not sin against thee" (Ps. 119:11).

Not only can we hide God's Word in our heart (life), but we can discover our life (heart) hidden in God's Word. When we realize the greatness of God in allowing our own life to bind with the Holy Scriptures in this way, we are encouraged and motivated to perpetually live within the constraints, or the "script" if you will, of the Scriptures.

I called out to God in my trouble, and He delivered me. He let me know that He was watching out for me by answering the underlying cry of my heart for spiritual salvation. He used the sound of thunder at the exact times so that I was forced to accept the fact that something supernatural was being conveyed to me. I was delivered from what should have been a routine conviction and prison term at my court martial in the army. I was in trouble just as it says in the verse, and at that time, I heard the first thunder. I was delivered immediately after I heard the thunder by the acquittal verdict.

Let me quote Psalm 81:7 one more time: "Thou calledst in trouble, and I delivered thee; I answered thee in the secret place of thunder: I proved thee at the waters of Meribah."

God led me to Washington. I know that because, first of all, it was there that I met the man whom I had nearly killed. It was four years after the court martial and about eight thousand miles away from our first encounter. Secondly, I know that God led me to Washington because that is where I found Him as my personal Savior.

According to the last part of Psalm 81:7, God said, "I proved thee at the waters of Meribah." I explained in a previous chapter how severely I was tried and tested early on in my Christian walk. Many times I thought that death was preferable to the unyielding harassment I endured, but instead I clung to Jesus with a death-grip.

As I studied about the waters of Meribah, I found that Moses was tested there with the unyielding harassment of the complaining Israelites. I had suffered similarly by my complaining wife. But God delivered me. He answered me by thunder and led me through the waters of Meribah where He proved my faith and commitment to Him—just as with Moses. I was severely tested in Moses Lake. This was my waters of Meribah. I'll repeat here a statement in *The Desire Of Ages*: "The experiences related in God's word are to be my experiences" (p. 390).

I believe God's chosen channel of communication to us is first and foremost through the Scriptures. We must have our spiritual ears open in order to discern specific instructions from God through His Word. Personal application of God's Word is what a personal relationship with Jesus is all about. I refer again to the statement on page 390 of *The Desire of Ages*: "We should carefully study the Bible, asking God for the aid of the Holy Spirit, that we may understand His word. We should take one verse, and concentrate the mind on the task of ascertaining the thought which God has put in that verse for *us*" (emphasis mine). In another place, the Spirit of Prophecy says we should study the Bible on our knees.

As a young lad Jesus discovered that His life was written in the Scriptures. It was so prophesied in Psalm 40:7, and in Isaiah 50:4-6, there is another prophecy of Jesus, which talks about His ears being opened: "he wakeneth morning by morning, he wakeneth mine ear to hear as the learned. The Lord God hath opened mine ear, and I was not rebellious, neither turned away back" (verses 4, 5).

We need to claim these promises for God to open our ears. Then we can hear God telling us the mystery of our mission. "If we come to Him in faith, He will speak His mysteries to us personally" (*The Desire of Ages*, p. 668). "Everyone needs to have a personal experience in obtaining a knowledge of the will of God. We must individually hear Him speaking to the heart" (*Ibid.*, p. 363). This should come about primarily through a study of the Scriptures since this is the first line of God's communication with us.

After my wife died and I began asking God if I could have a loving wife, God answered me through the Scriptures that I needed to wait for Him to teach me some things first. He did this by leading me to, and impressing upon me, the personal thought that He put in these scriptures for me: "And therefore will the Lord wait, that he may be gracious unto you, and therefore will he be exalted, that he may have mercy upon you: for the Lord is a God of judgment: blessed are all they that wait for him.... And though the Lord give you the bread of adversity, and the water of affliction, yet shall not thy teachers be removed into a corner any more, but thine eyes shall see thy teachers: And thine ears shall hear a word behind thee, saying, This is the way, walk ye in it." I quote here only a portion, but all of Isaiah 30:18-21 was impressed upon me.

Now the Lord revealed to me that my teachers were the Scriptures, particularly, but not limited to, the scripture promises that I was claiming.

I could expect, according to these passages quoted above, to hear God speaking to me His Word, in either direct quotes from the Bible or instructions that would be later confirmed by scriptures that He would lead me to. My "teachers" would no longer "be removed into a corner" when I learned the lessons connected with, and prerequisite to, receiving the gifts contained in the Scripture promises I was claiming. I would "see" my "teachers" when I received the gifts contained in the promises.

For example, the Lord spoke to me that I had better get used to enjoying the children's programs in church. Then He told me that I wasn't going to get off so easy as to have a wife with no children. Then He confirmed these instructions to me by leading me to this passage: "Yet setteth he the poor on high from affliction, and maketh him families like a flock" (Ps. 107:41).

Quite often now, when I have a question for God, I ask Him to answer me directly from the Scriptures. I hold my open Bible up in the air and say, "Talk to me Lord," and He does. I do not open randomly or poke my finger at the page with my eyes closed. It's not like throwing darts. I begin to look for scriptures that I think may have connection with my situation or question. Then the Holy Spirit leads me from one passage to another until I have my answer. I've also been awakened in the morning to find a scripture strongly impressed upon my mind. When this has happened, I often find that the message in the scripture fits the need that I have.

I had a tendency to forget the instructions God gave me or to discount them as a creation of my imagination. That's why I tried to pursue relationships with certain women, which didn't even go anywhere. After many months had passed and I was no closer to having a wife, or so it seemed to me, I came to these words in *The Desire of Ages*: "We are often led to seek Jesus by the desire for some earthy good; and upon the granting of our request we rest our confidence in His love" (p. 200). That's where I was stuck, and I knew it. But even the fact that I knew I was doing this and it was wrong didn't change my heart. I was hurt because the Lord hadn't given me a wife to heal my loneliness, and I clung to resentment toward Him. The statement goes on: "The Savior longs to give us a greater blessings than we ask; and He delays the answer to our request that He may show us the evil of our own hearts, and our deep need of His grace. He desires us to renounce the selfishness that leads us to seek Him" (*Ibid.*).

I knew I was delaying the answer to my request, but I couldn't seem to break out of my self-pity. I intellectually understood the lesson that the Lord was trying to teach me, but I wasn't receiving it into my heart.

Ellen White continues, "Not because we see or feel that God hears us are we to believe. We are to trust in His promises.... When we have asked for His blessing, we should believe that we receive it, and thank Him that we have received it. Then we are to go about our duties, assured that the blessing will be realized when we need it most. When we have learned to do this, we shall know that our prayers are answered" (*Ibid.*).

I read that statement for thirty days straight, but I still suspected the Lord of not wanting me to enjoy the pleasures of intimacy with a loving wife. I could see the evil of my own heart. I was withholding total love for the Lord until I should receive what I wanted. Satan had me believing that it was God withholding His love from me. The Lord was preparing me to better appreciate the gift when I should receive it, even though I was causing the delay in receiving it.

I see now my mistake. It is summed up well in this statement from *The Desire of Ages*: "We should not present our petitions to God to prove whether He will fulfill His word, but because He will fulfill it; not to prove that He loves us, but because He loves us" (p. 126).

This statement and the last one go along with a quote I saw on a wall plaque in the home some friends. It says, "Faith is not knowing God can do something, but that He will do something."

After I had been to Eastern Europe twice and had met a woman I thought I wanted to marry, I thought it would be nice to live in her country for about a year before bringing her and her son to America.

I presented my desire to the Lord and asked Him if it was all right for me to live in Eastern Europe for a year. There was an opportunity for me to work for a private printing house owned by a Seventh-day Adventist. The printing house had burned down, and they needed help rebuilding it.

I asked the Lord, of course, to answer me from the Bible, primarily. I had been studying off and on over the years about character development in relation to the twelve tribes of Israel. The twelve tribes are used to describe the twelve divisions of the 144,000 believers who will live blameless lives through the great time of trouble. They will live to see Jesus return to the earth to gather His church.

I want to be one of the 144,000, and I can only hope and prepare so that it will be so. Though I can not know for certain if I will be one of them, nevertheless, I have found that the divisions of the tribes, with twelve thousand in each one, together, represent a more grand and complete view of the character of Christ than any one of them could singularly.

The tribes represent the unique circumstances and experiences needed to develop a Christ-like character. Those designated as among the tribe they parallel most in strengths and weaknesses are perfect in their sphere as Christ is in His, yet all of the tribes together give a final and fuller display of the love of God to the world. This testimony will be said of them, "See how they love one another!"

In comparing my life to the Word of God and watching the tests and experiences that have come my way, I have been led to conclude that the development of my character most closely resembles that of Joseph. Please understand that I do not think I am anywhere near being worthy to be classed with Joseph in faith and integrity, but I only know that I've been tested in ways similar to Joseph. It is not my intention here to try and prove this. It is really a spiritual and personal understanding between the Lord and I. I simply share what God has shared with me.

I have looked carefully at the various places in the Bible where Joseph is mentioned. I was looking closely at Psalm 81 because that is where I first found that the Lord had a plan for my life, even before I ever acknowledged Him as my Sovereign Master. Since I was looking for God to answer me from the Scriptures, I was open to His leading and revelation as I studied.

It is hard to explain how I know when a certain text or texts is the answer I'm waiting for from the Lord. I have no desire to fabricate an answer from God. I fear that well-meaning church members are going to accuse me of twisting the Scriptures to make them say what I want them to. That's not my purpose at all. Now I know that if God says "no" about something it's because He has something better planned for me. In fact, it's not really a "no" answer. It is rather, "Wait, and I will help you change your mind to ask for something better."

Sometimes I need more than just coming across a scripture that seems to fit what I was asking about. I want to be very sure of what the Lord's will is in the matter. I do not want to be capricious, arbitrary, or manipulative. Satan is ready and willing to answer those kinds of prayers. Therefore, I also ask for specific signs as Gideon did. In Judges 6:17 Gideon said to the Lord, "Shew me a sign that thou talkest with me." The Lord gave Gideon that sign by making fire come out of a rock and consuming Gideon's sacrifice. There are those who base their whole experience on signs. This is an error, especially when the signs lead them to believe and act contrary to God's expressed will in His Word.

In my case I asked God to show me His favor (or disfavor) in my request to live and work in Eastern Europe. I wanted to help Eugen rebuild the printing house that had burned down. The sign I requested was for Eugen to acquire another printing press and begin rebuilding the printing house. That sign came, but since there was the possibility of that happening anyway, I still looked for a direct reply from Scripture.

Why did I go to the trouble of getting the Lord's input in the matter with such certainty? I could have simply chosen to do this thing and went ahead with my plans, trusting that the Lord would bless and protect me since I was simply trying to serve Him to the best of my knowledge and ability.

My attitude about following Jesus in just that—I want to follow where He is leading. I heard or read somewhere that God doesn't want us to work for Him but with Him. I believe God has a plan A for each of us. Why should we move blindly and end up with plan B, C, or so on? I believe we can get very specific about learning God's purpose for us, but there is also a danger of going to extremes. We don't need to seek the Lord's will for permission to use the restroom or take our next breath. Yet, if we have a very open relationship with the Lord, we can simply ask Him to show us what is reasonable and prudent in getting His input on our choices. God may override our choices, but He usually lets us pursue them so that we grow and learn from our mistakes. If our choices are wise, we still grow and learn. We learn how to continue to make choices consistent with the Lord's favor and blessing

As I was reading about Joseph in the Bible, I was especially interested to see that he is mentioned in Psalm 81. Now remember, I was specifically looking for an answer as to whether or not it was right for me to go live in Eastern Europe for one year. In verses 3 through 5 it says, "Blow up the trumpet in the new moon, in the time appointed, on our solemn feast day. For this was a statute for Israel, and a law of the God of Jacob. This he ordained in Joseph for a testimony, when he went out through the land of Egypt: where I heard a language that I understood not."

As I read these verses to ascertain the thought that the Lord had put in them for me, I found some interesting principles. God made it a law for Israel to blow trumpets in certain ways at certain times. There is much present truth embedded in symbolism in verse 3, but I won't go into detail about that now. It is blatantly obvious to me that blowing the trumpet represents giving a testimony of the Lord's grace in one's life. From these verses I gathered that the giving of testimony applied in a special way to the person of Joseph especially as it related to his experiences in Egypt.

Since I tend to identify with Joseph, I asked God what was in these verses for me in my relationship with Him in character development and in my mission for Him.

I had become disillusioned with the prison work, and for various reasons I believed God was weaning me away from that mission. Now I believed God wanted me to have a family and minister to troubled families and lonely and sick individuals. Psalm 107:41-43 says, "Yet setteth he the poor on high from affliction, and maketh him families like a flock. The righteous shall see it, and rejoice: and all iniquity shall stop her mouth. Whoso is wise, and will observe these things, even they shall understand the lovingkindness of the LORD." This helped me to understand, along with my study of the life of Enoch, how to develop a Christ-like character as a husband and a father while ministering to individuals.

I know that the Lord has given me an individual testimony that I love to share. I have shared it many times in a variety of places.

I then asked the Lord if, in addition to working for the printing house in Eastern Europe, I could share my testimony there. In Psalm 81:3-5 I received my answer to both requests. In verse 5 I understood that God had given me a testimony—"This he ordained in Joseph for a testimony." I was to share my testimony in Egypt, which, for me, meant Eastern Europe. Notice in the next part of verse 5 the narrative shifts to the first person singular—"where I heard a language that I understood not."

In Eastern Europe I definitely would hear a language I understood not. Something more in the last part impressed itself upon me. As I studied the word "heard" in the Hebrew lexicon of *Strong's Exhaustive Concordance*, I learned that the word "heard" in that verse also means "to publish." God's reply to me revealed that it was pleasing to Him for me go to Eastern Europe for a year to help publish books in another language, which I still can hardly understand after having spent a year there.

I was able to share my testimony in a variety of ways while living there. I was invited to attend a youth camping trip for one week in the mountains. There I was asked to share my experiences around the nightly campfire. With hundreds of youth from different towns, I was able to make many friends. It was one of the best weeks of my life.

I was privileged to speak at two public high schools in different towns. This was one of the most personally rewarding events of my life.

Another reason I had to be very sure it was in harmony with God's overall plan for my life to go to Eastern Europe for a year is because I was forced, by doing so, to quit the most lucrative and prestigious job I had ever had.

As I look back on all of the things the Lord taught me and did for me in Eastern Europe, I know without a doubt that He led me there. It was in Eastern Europe that the Lord chose to heal me of a severe digestive problem that had plagued me for many years. It was caused by a toxic and enlarged liver. I had prayed for years for healing. I spent thousands of dollars of personal money and even more of insurance money to no avail. I had many sophisticated tests done in America to find the problem. The doctors in America concluded their efforts by telling me my problem was "only imaginary."

It took a little old man working out of a rundown little clinic in an obscure little town to find the problem. He was a doctor who used natural remedies and medicines. He said I could pay him whatever I wanted for the treatment.

It was in Eastern Europe that God restored my respect for the leaders of my church. God used pastors, an evangelist, and church members to deliver me from what would have undoubtedly been another miserable marriage. Instead, I found a mate who gave me years of peace and comfort. God used faulty people like myself to help guide me along the right course.

There was a danger in the very process of trying to discern God's will for my life. The danger was this: I was believing that I had found the way to know God's plans for me, and I didn't have to respect the opinions and counsel of church leaders, or anyone else, concerning me. But God impressed upon me this thought in Proverbs 15:22: "Without counsel purposes are disappointed: but in the multitude of counsellors they are established."

I had, or thought I had, good reasons to despise the counsel and/or efforts of many leaders or members of our church. I saw in them what I believed was compromise and a watered-down message. They weren't following all of the counsels of the Bible and Spirit of Prophecy as I understood them.

But God used church leaders and other members to protect me from my own stupidity. I would have entered into an unwise marriage had not they faithfully warned and entreated me not to.

Then Lana made her definitive decision to follow Christ all the way through the efforts of church leaders and the appeals of evangelist Mark Finley. I must admit I could feel a strong presence of the Holy Spirit in his messages and appeals.

It was right around the time of those meetings and shortly afterward that I asked God very earnestly if He would bring me a wife soon. My time remaining in Eastern Europe was dwindling down. I knew that it had to be in Eastern Europe where I would find the kind of woman I was looking for. I was still desperately lonely. I asked God to tell me very specifically if the time was near for the fulfillment of my request.

I asked God to answer me from His Word. The Lord led me to a Scripture promise that I could claim as an answer to my heart's desire. I began claiming Jeremiah 33:14. It says, "Behold, the days come, saith the Lord, that I will perform that good thing which I have promised unto the house of Israel and to the house of Judah."

The Seven Thunders

That includes me because I am a spiritual Israelite according to Romans 2:29 and Galatians 3:29.

Now I had God's pledge that He would keep His promise to me for a wife and that the days for this were near.

Even after I had this answer, my faith wavered. There was still a delay. I knew that I had learned some of the lessons the Lord needed to teach me before I was consumed with the cares and responsibilities of having a wife. I went through an experience like Abraham who thought that God had forgotten His promise to him for a son from Sarah.

I continued to pursue relationships with women who had never been married. Yet the Lord hadn't forgotten His promise to me. It was I who had forgotten that the Lord indicated to me that I would receive a ready-made family. In other words, I would marry a woman with children already.

In order for me to have the kind of respect for a wife as a man ought to have, the Lord had to teach me one more lesson. These women made it quite clear to me that they were too pure for someone like me who had been in so much sin. I'm sure that wasn't the only reason they rejected me; nevertheless, they gave off an influence of pride that repulsed me. I'm not making a general statement about pure, virtuous ladies, mind you. I see it this way; I had just enough disgust from the women I pursued at that time to appreciate with the utmost respect a woman, who, like Lana, had been married once and had been faithful and pure in her loyalty.

I told in a previous chapter about the butterfly and my last rejection just at the time I met Lana. Just prior to this when things still didn't look too promising for a wife, I implored the Lord to let me know if the time was really here for me to find a woman who was serious about marrying me.

I told the Lord I understood that the days had come for Him to perform that good thing He promised me as I had claimed in Jeremiah 33:14. Unfortunately, that was too vague for me. I wanted to know what that meant. After all, a thousand years is as a day to God. Abraham waited twenty-five years for the fulfillment of His promise. "I don't have twenty-five years, Lord," I said. My time left in Eastern Europe was almost over, and with the end of the millennium near, I expected the time of trouble to start soon. "I'll never know a happy marriage in this life," I lamented to myself. My faith was hanging by a thread. I refused to let go of the angel, just like Jacob. My supposed enemy must become my friend.

"I must know that God answers His promises, not to prove He loves us but because He loves us," I told myself. "Lord, is the time now or isn't it?" I looked to the Bible for His reply. When the Spirit of Prophecy says that in reading the Bible it is as though we are in the very audience chamber of the Most High, I believe it.

My answer came as I was reading my Bible. I was led by the Holy Spirit to Jeremiah 1:11, 12: "Moreover the word of the Lord came unto me, saying, Jeremiah, what seest thou? And I said, I see a rod of an almond tree. Then said the Lord unto me, Thou hast well seen: for I will hasten my word to perform it."

I had my answer, without a doubt, but I have found that God always provides a lesson with answers and gifts. I looked further into the meaning of those two verses.

God asked Jeremiah what he saw. He saw the rod of an almond tree. God told him he had seen well because God would hasten His Word to perform it.

That experience was mine because God showed me the rod of an almond tree in principle. The rod of an almond tree is analogous with Aaron's rod that budded and bore almonds. This God did to impress the children of Israel with the validity of the leadership of the church. God did that for me. The circumstances were different for me, but the experience was the same because the same principle had to be taught to me.

I had harbored feelings of resentment toward my church family. I thought they merely tolerated me, and I alienated myself from them for a long time. Perhaps there were some members who resented my efforts to bring them into line. I think that I was of a wrong spirit in times past as I presumably sought to rebuke their transgressions. I did feel unwelcome at times around the church socials. My own discontent from not having a happy marriage had been reflecting back to me in other people's attitudes toward me.

Joseph had a little problem after receiving his coat of many colors. He felt a little bit favored instead of humbled by his blessing from his father. As a result, he was separated from his brothers and family. I had not been humble. I had not been ready to lay down my life for those I sought to correct. I have learned that I need correction and counsel as much, if not more, than anyone. I see in my own experience a parallel to that of Joseph who was separated from his brothers.

Lately, in asking God if I could move to the jungle of Borneo where Julie lives, I looked for my answer in the experience of Joseph. There I found this statement contained in the blessing that Moses pronounced on Joseph and his posterity, "And for the precious things of the earth and fulness thereof, and for the good will of him that dwelt in the bush: let the blessing come upon the head of Joseph, and upon the top of the head of him that was separated from his brethren" (Deut. 33:16). I hadn't realized that Joseph dwelt in the bush, but there it was, and the Lord was talking to me because I had specifically asked Him a question. How true it will be when I return to live in Borneo where I will enjoy the precious things of the earth and the fullness thereof in the bush. I will be separated from family and friends back here in America, but I will be living with the knowledge that I am living in God's will.

Over the years as God has broken my heart, my fiery misguided zeal has been healed. My accusatory tones have been replaced by those more in tune with entreaty. I have discovered weaknesses in myself and my need of love and support from my spiritual family. There has been reconciliation. I was overwhelmed with a sense of the willingness to forgive by my brothers and sisters in Christ. When I appealed to my church family for financial support to work in Eastern Europe for a year, they came forth with thousands of dollars and words of blessing and encouragement. God used them to facilitate the process of me finding my "butterfly" on the other side of the world. Joseph found his "butterfly" in Egypt far from his native home.

There is one more important lesson from the rod of the almond tree. When God caused Aaron's rod to bud and produce almonds, it was a miracle that a dead branch came to life again. Just as important, though, was the rapidity with which it took place. Spirit of Prophecy makes careful mention of this fact.

When all of the prerequisites are accomplished, God works quickly. When the Lord told me that I must wait in Isaiah 30:18-21, it was because He was waiting for me. Because of the waiting, it says, "therefore will he be exalted" (verse 18). It is true. The Lord used the delay to teach me inestimable lessons. These lessons increased my capacity to appreciate the gift of my wife. Because I appreciate this gift more now than I would have at an earlier time, it will return to God in a more exalted testimony from my mouth and pen—"therefore will he be exalted."

May God be exalted in my testimony and the experiences I've had throughout my life. May He be lifted up because of His goodness and graciousness to us, His children.

****

In light of what I have shared with you in this book of my life, do you doubt God's care for your every need? You needn't.

At last, I leave you with these questions: Do you believe you can trust the God I've described you? If so, then what do you want to do with your life, and what are you waiting for?

We invite you to view the complete
selection of titles we publish at:

www.TEACHServices.com

Scan with your mobile
device to go directly
to our website.

Please write or email us your praises, reactions,
or thoughts about this or any other book we publish at:

TEACH Services, Inc.
P U B L I S H I N G
www.TEACHServices.com

P.O. Box 954
Ringgold, GA 30736

info@TEACHServices.com

TEACH Services, Inc., titles may be purchased in bulk for
educational, business, fund-raising, or sales promotional use.

For information, please e-mail:

BulkSales@TEACHServices.com

Finally, if you are interested in seeing
your own book in print, please contact us at

publishing@TEACHServices.com

We would be happy to review your manuscript for free.

www.ingramcontent.com/pod-product-compliance
Lightning Source LLC
Chambersburg PA
CBHW081924170426
43200CB00014B/2821